Musings on Music: 1

## Forthcoming

Musings on Music Bk2: Philosophy and History

A Little Book of Poems

And Then? A Perception of the Path of Our Culture

Unexpected Places: Experiencing the Imaginal World

# Musings on Music

## Bk 1: Life and Composing

Clement Jewitt, PhD

Greenleaves

Published by Greenleaves, 2023
email: notinototherthanmecj@duck.com

ISBN: 978-0-9930621-1-7

Permissions received from:
Severnside Composers Alliance Newsletter (Chs 5 & 6, reworked)
Scientific and Medical Network Review (Ch. 9, reworked)
Music & Psyche Journal (Chs 8 & 11, reworked, and Appendix 3)

*Dedicated to all those who influenced what I have become:*
*Parents, family, friends, enemies, colleagues, tutors, villains,*
*spiritual leaders, lovers—welcomed or recoiled from,*
*all have played a part in moulding my clay.*

*With much gratitude to my wife Margaret who with these*
*good friends and colleagues have helped me create this book:*
*Deirdre Burton, Sarah Verney and Geoffrey Poole.*
*They have taught me the inestimable values of friendship.*
*And with particular gratitude to singer Wendy Nieper,*
*who has sung my songs so professionally,*
*and so beautifully.*

# Contents

Introduction     i

1. The nature of musical composition, and the joys of improvisation.   1

2. On being a late starting composer: An autobiographical note.    13

3. Composing: what music, and how? What are my compositional
    leanings?     25

4. Time or space: a note on modality and traditional Indian music, and
    its usages in my own composing work.     41

5. Sectio aurea? Fibonacci? Who cares ... ? An aspect of all composers'
    work.     49

6. How do we hear dissonance? A note.     57

7. What price another Way? Musings on life and music at the death of
    Boulez.     67

8. Jonathan Harvey. *In quest of spirit: thoughts on music.* Review.    77

9. Participative Spiritual Inquiry and the Music & Psyche enterprise.87

10. Spirit in music: a preliminary to Ch.11.     103

11. Musicmaking and healing the breach: mythmaking, synaesthesia,
    and the power of sound.     109

*Appendices*

1. Jewitt Family.     139

2. 70th Birthday Celebration Concert.     143

3. Three composers muse on life & Western art music.     149

*Encomiums and reviews.*     161

*Score samples.*     167

*Recordings references.*     183

*Bibliography.*     199

*Index of names.*     205

# Introduction

Music, being identical with Heaven, isn't a thing of momentary
thrills. or even hourly ones. It's a condition of eternity.

*Gustav Holst in a letter to a friend*

THIS IS THE FIRST OF TWO SHORT BOOKS in which I have put
together various thoughts and descriptions of matters concerning, principally, my own excursions into the world of
sound, both creatively as a composer and sometime performer,
and thoughtfully as a writer, together with some observations
concerning wider elements and contexts of what is a natural
part of every healthy human being's life as lived: music.

Spontaneous or pre-organised, bursting into song, or
energetically banging a drum, solitarily or as part of a group,
playing for ourselves or to audiences, all these are life-giving
actions, creating feelings, becoming emotions: living positively.

Just hearing the natural sounds around us, out of doors in
our gardens or walking in the woods, such as insects buzzing,
birds chirping, shrieking or croaking, the rustle of the wind in
the trees and the undergrowth, and maybe the odd fox or other
larger animal calling its own directed or undirected messages,
all this, taken as it comes, is music, world music in the widest
possible connotations.

In a relaxed state, freeing ourselves from past anxieties and
future fears, receptive to the present moment, we can with all

possible feelings reach out to and receive reciprocally all these natural vibrational evidences of LIFE, the living universe.

However we humans are also inventive: we create.

As do some other creatures. Blackbirds, among others, transcend the merely formulaic though nevertheless appealing songs of many feathered folk. And other creatures also have creative soundings as an integral part of how they live: Whales in particular make long extensive songs, wonderfully emotive to the human hearer, with which to contact brethren, who may be very far distant, songs sent through their watery medium, further than we can send sounds through the airy medium.

In many and varied ways we appreciate the inventions of our human brethren, as well as those of other creatures. So, we in the modern world listen, to suit our preferences, to the live and recorded musics readily available. And we sing in choirs, play instruments in bands and orchestras: these may be pre-written pieces to fit established voice and instrumental groupings, or may be improvisatory endeavours for those who are inclined to participate in the immediacy of creativity in the sounding moment..

Much of this is alluded to in the writings in this little volume, which were put together for differing purposes over more than a couple of decades. Since my own principal focus has been for some years, decades, working on musical composition, the first two chapters briefly introduce my attitudes toward life and activities in order to suggest the origins of my musical proclivities, sitting atop, perhaps, or within, the allusions presented in the previous paragraphs above.

This is followed by some amplifications evincing philosophical and musical ruminatory perceptions, indicating something of the detailed nature of my approach to composition, including the influences of classical Indian music, which naturally bears on the composed outcomes.

Some account is also presented of the informalities of improvisation, a rather beautiful separate musical activity from formal pre-composition, tending seemingly towards more traditional musical forms.

The last and largest chapter is essentially an extended paean in praise of music making, whether formally or informally, as a necessary human, individual and cultural binding force.

In support of the main texts, some Appendices follow: a note on my creative ancestry; reports on a birthday celebration concert, and musical musings with two composing friends, first created as a three way emails exchange. Writings by others about my work as a composer follow, and some sample scores for those who wish to read them.

Then there are recordings, some specifically noted in the main texts, some not. The book publishing habit here used to be the inclusion of a CD: however, that medium is seemingly becoming passé, and I note that many of my friends no longer have a disc player, except in their cars. So I have placed chosen recordings on the web, with links to access them and amplificatory and song texts placed within the *Recordings references* Appendix: https://clementjewitt.co.uk/

Musings on Music Bk. 2 will consist of less personal, somewhat more objective historical-philosophical work, including a wished for future for all the arts, sonic healing modalities, Western music history placed in a Jungian framework, music at the Bauhaus, a not too deep psychological investigation of the characters in *The Magic Flute* and how they interact, and some scattered writings from book reviews and other projects.

June 2023

One

# The nature of musical composition
# and the joys of improvisation

*See deep enough, and you see musically; the
heart of Nature being everywhere music.*
*Thomas Carlyle*

AFTER SEVERAL DECADES WORKING at finessing formal composing, I had experienced a sufficient amount of performances (even famous composers have unplayed works) and had some satisfying recordings made. This active participation in the highly structured formal mainstream—submissions to performers, competitions and so on—had resulted in somewhat occulted movements up or down the ladder of status in the British 'new music' world. All *seemingly* well. Perhaps I had not paid proper attention to the matter of that 'status'! Not my perception of necessity.

But then another aspect of music making overtook me. In my eightieth year I put down all formal performing and composing in favour of working improvisationally with one of my lifetime abiding loves: trees. In a leafy wood, the resultant heard sound is rather different from that in even the best acoustically organized concert hall, which aims at spreading the sound evenly across the audience. Rather, many thousands of leaves are arbitrarily redirecting the sound in many directions.

The result is a kind of sonic mist, audible seemingly on occasion over quite wide distances within the natural silences of the wood.

Playing *with* rather than *at* trees in a wood often provides some inner perception of response. This may be no more than a faint feeling indicating acceptance: the trees seemingly appreciate being played to—or is it the tree devas responding?

As an example, in a remote part of the grounds of Gaunt's House in Dorset, where I was at a week long teaching on Inka Spiritualities, I found a venerable old plane tree, which seemed to me to be the twin, or double, of a similar ancient I had once come across in a wood to the east of Birmingham. I had played to that, and now played to the one at Gaunt's, and was honoured both times by very clear unexpected warm feelings.

Two days later at Gaunt's I returned there, but didn't feel like playing immediately, so leaned against the trunk savouring the quiet rustling of leaves and the absence of anything other than 'nature'. Then I realised that the afternoon course session was near beginning, and got up to go. But ... a loud strong word filled my head: "Play!"[1] Not a command to be ignored. So I did, received a strong and very welcome feeling response, and was a little late for the session!

What is missing in the picture above (another occasion) is our little dog, who had ceased running about and was sitting quietly, listening, though out of the picture, And on yet another occasion, some cows in an adjacent field stopped grazing and came to stand by the fence while I played; and once when I played from a stationary canal boat while companions were refilling the water tanks, a family of mallards paddled over to be right by the boat.

Making contact with our fellow earthly creatures is very heartwarming.

❖   ❖   ❖   ❖   ❖

## COMPOSING AND BEING A MUSICIAN

THERE IS A SIGNIFICANT COMMON FACTOR in the processes in which I worked during my life: architectural design, computer system specification, and of course musical composition. In all three, a large number of discrete elements are required to be creatively assembled into a coherent form within the differing

---

1    I shall not attempt any 'explanation'.

boundaries of possibilities and functions pertaining to each discipline. That relates to the dimension of thinking, as serving the craft element. In addition, architecture requires for good results at the least a visual æsthetic, and composition naturally requires an auditory æsthetic—I will leave the elusive concept of 'æsthetics' undefined here: readers will I expect have their own sufficient and overlapped views.

In my own experience, musical composition comprehensively and primarily involves feeling and intuition, though thinking is indeed then required for the transfer of compositional visions onto the score, whether physical or electronic. Additionally to those, therefore, is necessarily required the spiritual as carrier of value and meaning. These aspects were lacking in the utilitarian creation of computer systems, though that was at least intellectually satisfying.

How can composing *not* be the best work to do !

However, formal composing—producing scores for others to read, interpret and perform—is not enough. Some practical experience in performing is crucial to really being a musician. *Inter alia* I have always found writing for piano somewhat tricky—I am not, I realize, a sufficiently practiced pianist! Consequently there are few piano works in my portfolio.

So, in addition to the choral singing and local brass band experiences, which latter taught me some valuable early lessons in ensemble work, I did some solo singing with my tenor voice, founded a mostly baroque music occasional ensemble with my friend and colleague, pianist Mike Bardsley (recorders, harpsichord, singers and continuo), a chamber choir consisting of all the local soloists in North Oxfordshire, and informally taught classical guitar and occasionally other instruments. While at Birmingham Conservatoire taking my BMus I took an option on percussion playing, which I found valuably meaningful, not only for compositional purposes: the practice did help score writing, though rather elusively that value seems more than somewhat beyond verbal exposition.

But the formality of all such work also needs a balancing compensation, which I found in the inestimably valuable personal experience of a performance by sitarist Ravi Shankhar, that truly great classical Indian musician, whose concert performances drew audience members out of any time consciousness (*extempore* indeed) into their own extended timeless moments.

The Royal Festival Hall was absolutely crammed. After a while when Ravi had got going, I, and I feel sure all others, simply lost awareness of fellow audience members, aware only of the all pervasive sounds which seemed to enter into us so magically, emanating from that figure on the stage, but seeming to come from nowhere. The supporting duo, on tabla and tamboura, were surely there, but I have absolutely no memory of them. Time passed, much time passed, but we were, collectively I think, not aware of it. Did he keep to the time allotted by the Festival Hall? I have no idea. When we all tumbled out afterwards, the world seemed to be different, alien, needing to be readjusted to, re-found anew.

That particular night at a now forgotten date in the 1960s remains still a personal bench mark by which to measure the extent of my engagements with and responses to other performances, of whatever kind. Few have even approached it, in my perceptions.

Which brings in innovatory psychologist C.G. Jung's attitude to music. In 1956 he was visited by concert pianist Margaret Tilly, who had contacted him with regard to her interest in music therapy. She reported that he greeted her with delightful interest in what she could tell him about herself. In the conversation he noted that he had ceased listening to music: "I never listen to music any more. It exhausts and irritates me." Why so? "because music is dealing with such deep archetypal material, and those who play don't realize this".[2] Of course that reply does not necessarily apply to all players, though I concur that many, maybe most, musicians do not get up to, let alone beyond, their own personal physical, feeling and emotional limits.

I would propose both Josef Szigeti and Pablo Casals as instrumentalists projecting deep soul connections into their music, beyond the personal. And among ensembles, the old

---

2  Tilly 1977 IN *CG Jung Speaking*

Quartetto Italiano half a century ago: Late photographs of them show clearly to my eye the physical effects of profound and unending searching for the authenticity, the reality to the composers' intentions lying hidden in the material of the presented score, in their performances, which to my ear they achieved much more than most.

I recall a talk I gave on the meaningfulness of, and in, music to first year students at the Birmingham Conservatoire, in which reportedly I had successfully avoided turning the philosophy into a dusty dryness ! One of those freshers had signed up for the BMus course in the expectation that he would make money as a nicely trained pop band musician—an inevitable aspiration in the materialist culture we live in. He was quite perky about the intention. At the end of the talk he was looking thoughtful. A few days later he told me he might want to change his direction. I told him who to talk to. My perception was that he was perhaps realising his own deeper potentials, though I imagined that he who had accepted him as a student had divined it. I'm not against pop music *per se* ! What best fits, go for !

Much work occurred in and beyond the Conservatoire, including that with musical friends interested in the more esoteric aspects of music-making. We founded a group, *Music & Psyche*, devoted to encouragement of what we may call a shared spontaneity in all comers to our weekend workshops, via improvisation.[3]  So I became an enthusiastic improviser, after transcending my fear of losing the musical direction in the performing moment, a fear experienced by I imagine most classically trained musicians in modern times !

As I gradually discerned, there is no 'wrong' note in free improvisation.  Each musical utterance carries within it many potentials.  The player learns, or rather the players learn, collectively by pre-sharing feelings, not at all necessarily by overt discussion, to choose a direction in the sounding moment. and additionally, a precognition, which a traditionally convinced materialist would instantly attempt to explain away.  But I experientially know the difference between a choice of overall musical direction taken before beginning and an unexpected route emerging in advance of the moment of playing it, whether lead by me or by another participant who, as often happens, had simultaneously picked up the new musical direction.

Similarly, the milieux of traditional jazz expects solos to develop from what has been announced by the band as a whole, but even so a precognition as I attempted to define it here can also emerge, though inflected by the pre-determined origin—*this* is what creates a really magical improvisation.

Ravi Shankhar primarily worked his magic spells from extended improvisations subsequent to 'announcing' the music

---

3  See Ch 8  in this volume.

(which is what indicates the similarity in overall structures between classical Indian music and Jazz), often no more (no more?) than elaborate explorations of the intervallic structures of the *rāg* in use (note and intervals sequences), sometimes extended far beyond most hearers focussed hearing capacity: the timelessness of the extended moment.[4]

There is a story whose authenticity I do not know, amusingly illustrating this. At a recital, his totally absorbed improvisation continued beyond an hour (it was reported). One by one, the audience left as their endurance found limits, until there was just one person remaining. After a while Shankhar noticed, stopped playing, and asked "Why are *you* still here?", to which the man replied "You are sitting on my rug!"

❖   ❖   ❖   ❖   ❖

AND NOTWITHSTANDING THE EVENTS OUTLINED ABOVE, I have something similar to the Haydn problem. When he retired, he became plagued by musical ideas, for as I understand it he no longer had the emotional or physical energy to summon up the requisite focussed concentration required to enable the felt, unasked for music 'delivered' to his conscious mind to be rendered into usable scores.

So it sometimes seems to be with me: and banal ditties are

---

4    See Ch.4 for a fuller discussion of Indian music.

also frequent, from too much 'public' electronic soundings galloping through the brain, alas ! Improvising and playing to the trees in the quietude of the wood is definitely the best recovery process for this old man.

And life goes on !

Two

## On being a late starting composer

I love music passionately, and because I love it I try to free it
from barren traditions that stifle it. It is a free art, gushing
forth—an open-air art, an art boundless as the elements, the
wind, the sky, the sea! It must never be shut in and become
an academic art.                                    *Claude Debussy*

THIS NOTE COMMENTS ON HOW I found and began to manifest
my innate musicianship.  Before that did so, though, other
creativities arose.  I took to drawing, sketching, quite early, my
sculptor grandfather's habit, though I have nothing saved done
in my childhood, for then I was more concerned with my
miniature railway. The two activities were paralleled, naturally,
and the sketching continued until a family began to grow.

The last sketch I did (on the previous page) was in 1970, of Shoreham in NW Kent viewed from half way up the valley side, with my wife and our first child asleep beside me.

During the decades of the 1970s-80s, when I was in my 30s & 40s, I developed an interest in early music, partly owing to a fascination with the high point of English music, in the 17thC, Elizabethan and Restoration times.

Learning to play a typical instrument of those times, the recorder, a term partly derived from cultural habits then of playing to caged birds,[1] was naturally followed by the acquisition of a consort of them, from the tiny sopranino, as small as my big fingers could manage, down to the bass, quite large with necessary right hand finger keys needed to accomplish the full pitch stretch. Those I acquired are all traditional wooden instruments, made in the old styles, underpinning for me professional level performance activity.

A parallel interest in the classical guitar was also present. I learned to master that considerably more complex instrument with lessons at the Spanish Guitar Centre in London. Then followed putting on concerts, mostly focussed on early music, but also on traditional and new Spanish and other music written for the guitar up to the 20thC, while living in the small town of Chipping Norton, Oxfordshire.

---

1  Aiming to induce the bird to focus on the tune by covering the cage with a thick cloth to limit the bird to hearing: 'recording' being the technical term at that time for learning.

During the course of my living and working as a composer and musician, I also acquired skills in other instruments: flute with a brief experiential touch, clarinet, brass, percussion, and the viola. The latter I had no intention of gaining sufficient skill in for performance, only learning to handle it for purposes of composition—to help me gain some understanding of the feasibility of hand moves on that family of instruments.

Much of these developments lead to involvements in concerts and recitals with various musicians in the County, and wider elsewhere.

❖   ❖   ❖   ❖   ❖

## LIFE STORY

THIS MINOR LIFE STORY has multiple origins—one is asked for something biographical on many occasions. For present purposes I have made a hopefully reasonable and not too egotistical amalgam of many such summaries. The writing here is best treated as a backdrop to all that follows.

In my twenties, musical performing was burgeoning, with others using my new bought recorders, and singing, chorally, and eventually occasionally solo. As a family began to form, though, less time was available for all my 'hobbies'—viewed as important to all I did, life-giving.

Meanwhile the practice of miniature construction, for my small scale railway, morphed into joinery, habitual in my family, and useful for setting up a home:  nearly all my bookshelves, occasional furniture including a bed long enough for my over six feet height, and a small traditionally styled oval table on a single leg, were among the items individualising various house moves. I still have and use a cabinet made by my grandfather.

The time needed for such work was not found later, which in the end did not matter, for the music became primary, and practice on my recorders became a useful way for settling the young children after their bed time stories, my tweeting wafting up the stairs: some of them recall this with affection.

My eldest daughter noticeably inherited that prolixity: she developed skills musically, and visually as a painter. Her story is left alone here, for her own depicting as she may.

For something on the origins of those multiple skills, see the Appendix: *Jewitt Family.*

Despite all that energetic activity, physical and other, simultaneously early trauma was limiting development, constricting a fully authentic life.

❖   ❖   ❖   ❖   ❖

BORN IN NORTH LONDON INTO an ordinary enough but modestly difficult family near the beginning of WW2, my accessible early memories are almost exclusively of bomb explosions, extensive fires, windows blown in, and houses become piles of rubble. And familiar people no longer visible, whose absences taught me the limits to physical life. Oh, and frightening aircraft noises and the moaning air-raid sirens of those times, which can still resuscitate an inescapable inner fear, experienced in history films. Later in the war came 'doodle-bugs', as they were referred to (unmanned bomb rocket planes), which we learned were about to fall when the droning ceased: their calculated fuel had run out—one hoped they were not close.

Nothing particularly unusual here, for those living at that time in the several UK cities experiencing bombing, though affects are partly a matter of how deeply such experiences drill into one's individual character and sensitivities—and age. Family history says that my sister (11 months older) cried most of the time. I, though, was expected to conform to the middle class cultural expectations of those times: Boys Don't Cry! She was somewhat processing the traumatic experiences; I was internalizing them in order not to display any feelings. We both manifested long term systemic outcomes, expressed differently according to our temperaments and how we were behaving during the experiences.

And I do not blame my mother for that expectation: she was following cultural norms, as many of us tend to do in the very much increased debilitating expectations we blindly follow eighty years later, triggered by inner processes bearing on humanities communal nature, governmentally denied.

Certainly this start cast a deep shadow over the first 40

years of my life: in adulthood I became a not quite total alcoholic, and a heavy smoker: perhaps fortunately nothing worse than tobacco came my way, though that can do plenty of harm if not organically grown. I tried a handful of career paths: architecture, librarianship (for the love of books), and the burgeoning computer world, each of which paths faltered and fell, for various reasons related to the handicaps noted.

However it wasn't totally bad, as despite the burdens I learned another couple of instruments, sang in choirs, and started a family with a wife coming out of a not dissimilar family constellation: We certainly, though unwittingly, gave our children stiff problems to surmount in their lives, alas! Looking back, I must have been quite largely running on automatic. Not possible to helpfully relate to children in really good emotive depth, nor yet to compose meaningfully ! Even though from time to time I felt an inner urge to compose, I could not during those years get any clear purchase on the necessities of the actual practice.

However, in the late 1970s a discovery occurred of a quite deep amnesia, which was revealed by a friend pointing out a building we were passing which he recalled I had worked in: at that time I had a completely blank memory of it. On careful inner reflection following the incident I discovered that I had blotted out most of my earlier life. Occasionally memories still return at this time of writing: sometimes being the release of unconsciously buried childhood trauma.

As an example, the last to occur was in 2022, totally out of the blue, which had me running home from the dentist, astonished at my unexpected fearfulness. It took till a blocked memory arose during that night's sleep to understand, early the next morning: a memory from probably aged 3, or maybe 4, of being in a circle of adults, towering above me, all of whom were wearing gas masks, which hung down like ghastly contorted elephant probosces, very different from the much smaller masks of the 2020s decade, but, *crucially*, also denying the perceived humanity of the wearer. More context on the event is still buried, though the trigger seems understandable in the context of mask wearing during the recent fear pandemic.

Continuing the narrative, a profound emotional collapse in 1981 signalled the beginning of the end of the troubles. For that breakdown proved to be a *breakthrough*, and a route to a better, more aware life came out of it. Psychologist Steve Taylor calls such events spiritual awakenings, or Transformation Through Trauma, which he notes can occur in shockingly immediate circumstances, such as unexpected deaths of loved ones, or from sustained experiences such as imprisonment.[2] And also from what I am indicating here, though he doesn't specifically mention it, from early decidedly unsettling life experiences which may well have been lost to conscious memory, released

---

2   see Taylor 2021

mysteriously by an unexpectedly contemporary situation or event, such as that narrated above: a similar visual or other 'echo'—a non-verbal metaphor of the original experience.

In the recovery from that I managed to stop the smoking, and (gradually) the drinking, simultaneously learning to live with a new and growing heart problem, which seemed to me to be the early trauma and behavioural expectations laid on me finally manifesting in my body—soma follows psyche.

As an illustration of that process, but not here presented as a strict parallel, German Jews who had escaped from the Nazis to the USA reported similarly after they had retired: the traumas they had experienced had first been covered over by settling into a new life, focussed on forming new social connections, working and rearing families. Then, following the relaxation consequent on retirement, came dire recollections, reflected in reports of psychotherapeutic activity in New York in the 1970s/80s.

Hindsight suggests that such experiences should be taken to be, viewed from the overall span of a long and meaningfully experienced life, not tragic, but a circumstantial requirement which predicates in the end necessary inner growth. Which we may say we came to this planet to experience, however long within the lifetime that may take to manifest. We all live our lives uniquely: some of us find our feet earlier than others, some never do in their current particular incarnation. Taylor's discussion in the book noted above was very helpful, in effect rather astonishingly, or perhaps not so, acting as to some extent a resumé of my own early life.

Fortuitously in the early 1980s I was made redundant from career number three (early computer industry), for this gave me the space to begin to try out composing, as an autodidact, initially for the instruments I was playing: classical guitar, brass, and recorders. Local musicians were supportive, particularly harpsichordist Mike Bardsley, who became a close friend, always ready to participate in performances. Some composing opportunities occurred: music for a community play; a prize in the Oxford music festival for a brass quartet; and other small encouragements.

All good so far, but I realised that I needed to be officially 'educated', for several musicians experiencing my compositions had enquired "Where were you trained?" So I began checking out various possibilities. The big London Schools on visits felt depressingly like morgues, so I backed straight out; and the interviewer at Bristol University seemed to fear the possible rebellious individualist attitude of someone considerably older than he ! So I chose, and so entered, the Birmingham Conservatoire, which had a large School of Composition, and an active World Music Department, both of which were definite attractions. Meanwhile all my four children had grown and gone, along with their mother, who sadly had died of cancer.

At Birmingham I first gained a BMus, then went straight on to Research level, at the instigation of the Director of Studies, who then anxiously asked "You *do know* the Philosophers?" I lied, and made a mental note: do some reading ! And I did.

❧   ❧   ❧   ❧   ❧

DURING ALL THIS MY HEART PROBLEM GREW, peaking in the late 1990s. The medics offered me Warfarin, which I refused on the grounds that I am not a rat ! I had been uneasy about conventional medicine for some years: too many large scale problems have come out of it—and too much focus on pathogens, not enough on variable susceptibility, nor on relevant personal events in earlier and current life, not often asked about.

The heart problem has been gently reducing since then. It is not now a *disease* requiring attention from eager allopathy, but just a personally manageable *attribute*, controllable via breath work, much to the disbelief of some traditionally orthodox medics !

In the next four chapters we will explore the types and aspects of music which have attracted me in the context of my composing. We will survey some of the ways I have viewed that work: full frontal, and sideways, glancings looking at aspects of the compositional enterprise—time spans, proportions, and hard or softly organised for audition.

# Three

## Composing: what music, and how?

*The real voyage of discovery consists not in
seeking new lands but in seeing with new eyes.*
*Marcel Proust*

AT A DINNER PARTY WITH a group of lovely people I had not
met before, gathered for an exploration of the spiritual connectivities of English West Country ancient monuments, I was
asked "Who is your favourite composer?" After mentally
recalling all the many composers who taught me something,
and whose music has for me abiding meaningfulness, I realised
that I could not single out any one of them, not even Beethoven
or J.S. Bach, though both of those two came to occupy peaks in
the landscape of my musical experiences. And so, somewhat
reluctantly, I realized that there was only one possible answer to
the question: ME !

Which perhaps smacks of egoism, or at least much self con-
fidence. But if we don't like what we do, why are we doing it?

❖   ❖   ❖   ❖   ❖

COMPOSING OUTLOOK

FROM THE TIME OF DECIDING that it was possible to work at
musical composition (during recovery from my breakthrough

experience: see Ch. 2) I had felt my way experientially through listening to traditional jazz, playing with brass bands, in which I had played on the tuba, and the delights of early music, which I also participated in with my consort of recorders, and also Spanish guitar recitals. Later I started attending 'new music' concerts, *de rigueur* for a would be modern composer !

Sometime during these experiences of increasing musical understanding there occurred a magic moment, as meaningful as the earlier Ravi Shankhar experience, noted in Ch.1. The music of J.S. Bach 'spoke' to me: the clarity of that in the revelatory moment was extraordinary, a true widening and deepening of consciousness. This was not merely momentary, but stayed with me, and still does, a permanent inner growth which sprang out of a singular happening. Not uncommon, for it is one of the ways in which, often unexpectedly, spiritual growth occurs.

That experience was confirmation of the decision to compose.

I had comprehensively listened up the history line from 12$^{th}$C France to the early 20$^{th}$C wider Europe: Composers Debussy, Bartok, Mahler, Holst, Britten and Shostakovich came to my expectant ears. To determine what more contemporary composers were doing I took my listening further into the 20$^{th}$C. All the innovators: Schoenberg, Webern, Stravinsky (after waiting for Schoenberg's death—to avoid competing I believe),

Birtwistle, Berio, Ligeti, Messiaen, Stockhausen, Takemitsu, etc.

Too many but certainly not all the developments entered into by those composers were in my hearing largely intellectualised and *not felt*: definitely children of the age of the primacy of intellectualism which we are not yet fully beyond, so shadowing out intuition as the necessary handmaiden of creativity, and in parallel tending to cut off the heart, and so feelings, or aspects of that at least, seemingly out of unspoken irrational fear of reverting to 19thC. Romanticism: mustn't regress, we humans always surpass our ancestors, do we not? Hmm !

Thus the condition of our age, then peaking, lead to the alienation of much of the listening public in the 1950s and 60s. More recently some welcome *rapprochement* between contemporary composers and audiences is evident, both sides, importantly, having shifted ground towards a mutual accommodation. Better if not viewed as *compromise* though: few *avant gardistes* would willingly accept that nomination !

But I was left with a personal problem. Too many perceptible differences among all those industrious innovators. I could not hope to follow all those leadings: not that I wanted to, except with respect to keeping an eye on the notion that *recognition* as a composer would require some obeisance to the main contemporaneous thrusts, in Great Britain at least: Apparently less so in North America.[1]

---

1   See Appendix 3.

But and however I never was a follower, so that had to go out the window or I risked losing my authentic musical self, only just recognised through the experience of the revelatory moment concerning J.S. Bach, noted above. And I realised that my sense of lyricism was going to have a hard time of it if I situated my work too firmly into high modernist atonality and serialism. I needed something else. I needed particularly, above all, to be myself!

The musical moment of any duration is always a triad: the composer, the performer, and the listener, combined in less than three persons or not. Without a listener there is no music, which assertion does perhaps suggest existentialism, or Buddhism! But I'll stay with it. With that triad in mind I came to the view that extreme atonalism/serialism was the end mark of an investigative enterprise that leaves the legacy of a set of useful compositional tools, one among other families of technique. And I could not entirely abandon tonality, owing partly to the acoustic reality of the traditional harmonic triad (notes C E G and related triplets), and partly to the need to feel culturally linked to the past, not bereft of my own and our culture's history. Thus I personally repudiate Pierre Boulez' ultramodernist project to disassociate 'new' music from the past.[2] Nothing springs unforeseen, without birth.

However, starting composing in middle age itself brings problems. Beginning near fifty constituted a definite late start

---

2 See Chapter 7 in this volume.

in the notoriously long composing apprenticeship—twenty years or so is hardly enough to develop really authentic music. Though of course we never stop learning, or we are effectively dead. The busy gate-keepers of contemporary music, mostly ensconced in the heights of academe, perforce are guided by assumptions: *Deep* score reading is a rarely well practiced and most definitely time consuming art. Faced with an unfamiliar name (or even scoring style, which *should* attract attention, but maybe not always does) youth is assumed, therefore youthful exuberance. If the latter is not perceptible in the score in hand, habitual ideology suggests that this 'youth' has nothing to mature with.

Which goes toward explaining why this 'youth' generally got his work rejected. Those who support my work are to a person uninvolved in the authoritarian mainstream of so called 'modern classical' music: They simply appreciate the depth of communication in mine, not visible to the busy gate-keepers hurriedly scanning scores, in the safe exclusionalities of academe.

An example of this process, perhaps, was my *Invocations to Archangels*, composed for the Orlando male vocal quartet at the invitation of the SPNM (Society for the Promotion of New Music),[3] which rejected it. The Orlandos loved it, and gave it its première at Dartington where they were teaching that year— unfortunately I was unable to be present, which I much regret.

3   *for the Prevention* in some views !

Later it was chosen to be broadcast on BBCr3 as representative of the pieces performed that summer in Dartington. What more could one want? A choral version has been sung several times to great acclaim, attracting heartening reviews.

The choral version seems to me to be more appropriate to the sung words, taking 'Archangel' to be the spiritual leader of a host of Angels ! Wherefrom did I get the theme? The venue which was to host performances of the resultant SPNM call for compositions was at that time displaying paintings by an artist specialising in angels. I decided to honour that in my piece, but further up the angelic hierarchy !

Several people have approved of it: "It seemed to me that, had he had access to modern composition techniques, William Byrd could have written this." *Andrew Burniston,*[4] Independent Jung scholar,[5] introducing me at a talk to the London Jung Club. And on the choral version: "With its constantly changing time signatures and subtle, shifting harmonies, this striking work has a mesmerising quality." *Neil Crutchley, Leicester Mercury.*

So, what were the SPNM people thinking? They denied having an agenda when I challenged them over also rejecting my PhD piece, *The Night Sea: Aspects of an ordinary life,*[6] for which assessors, including the composer Anthony Powers, had

4   Now Frederick, or Fred

5   That comparison created in me a truly heart rending feeling: Me ! compared with one of Englands greatest composers?

6   For solo female voice, male voice choir & 19 instrumentalists. Eight poems from 8 poets, plus one of my own, formed the 'story', encased in extensive instrumental poems: duration c.50'. See Score Samples.

not asked for alteration of a single note, and no less a contemporary figure than Jonathan Harvey had provided a fulsome endorsement:

> It's a powerful piece, I would love to hear it. It's an interesting form, balancing tensions and speeds convincingly, even without the psycho-spiral narrative! But as a marriage of music and textual journey it must be quite an experience.
>
> I was impressed by the economy and directness of the writing. In many movements (8 & 9 for instance) the repetitions take on a strong musico-ritualistic expression—which is different from the merely ritualistic ... These repetitions are never tiresome, on the contrary, they arouse interest in the larger span, and the movements are all quite terse without being mean; they have some generosity of expansion as well. The canonic stuff also strikes me as very beautifully calculated.

Alas, he never did hear it![7] One may speculate whether there is something in his thoughts bearing on my work, which indicates why his music was seemingly more respected on the continent than in the UK.

The comment by the Guardian critic on the 2000 SPNM/London Sinfonietta 'State of the Nation' weekend, that "there were 25 premieres, of which 24 might have been written by the same composer",[8] seems to point to a certain consensus of 'new music' composing. I still wonder who the 25th was: I should have investigated . . . It would seem that there is no real

---

7    Died 2012
8    Brought to my notice by colleague Maxwell Steer

official consensus in the 'styles' of contemporary music, just a collective conforming, perhaps more than probably largely unexamined, and similarly unconscious.

Perhaps there may be signs of change now, a widening out towards recognition of the validities of various 'styles', and therefore of individual autonomous workings, pointing necessarily to a loosening of former 'gatekeeping' strictures on style boundaries, signalling movement into a new Aeon, as C.G. Jung discussed profoundly, and composer Michael Tippett mused on in our field of music.[9]

One may recall the *avant-garde* criticisms of that great innovator Bartok's late work in America, as a regression from the adventurous sharp edges of previous work; and that Schönberg, had he lived longer, some think, may well have found compromises from total 12 tone work—his later works can seem to be heading that way. The point is that for most, if not all composers, life's stages are naturally reflected in their compositions:  the young strive for recognition, so typically work hard at novelty and the spectacular; the old at length may find something broader and deeper, needing not the youthful fireworks, though able to provide them if appropriate.  And in mature midlife? Perhaps some of my music provides a clue? [I refuse to be definitively classed as 'old'.  Not yet, anyway !]

The point here predicates on the extent of each persons inner development, governing how much compromise is

---

9    Jung CW 9ii. Tippett 1974

accommodated in the craving for public recognition. Our current dire culture is overfull of immature persons of all chronological ages. The validity and authenticity or not of all creative work reflects this: Intuition and feeling define, not always consciously. Hopefully we are indeed moving into the greater personal autonomy, and consequently and hopefully more flexible mutual acceptances, of the Aquarian age.

Further, there is another view to be taken here, which I pick up from George Hansen's in-depth critical examination of who occupies the margins of social structures, including shamans, healers, mediums, and the artistically creative—all who chafe against the increasingly strict and increasingly bureaucratically enforced social structures. As all of that increases, the freedom of creatives becomes progressively compressed and margin-alised: Could a new Beethoven succeed now? This ongoing cultural restrictioning may well be another reason why the new music gatekeepers fail to perceive any depths in a score? Hansen emphasises that these progressive tightenings are invisible to most—timescales of change are long, and auto-induced cultural proclivities too unnoticed.[10]

❖　❖　❖　❖　❖

THREE WORDS COME UP again and again in appreciations of my music. "Your music is evocative and haunting. It has a myster-ious quality"; "The music is evocative and haunting."; "this

---

10　Hansen 2001

hauntingly beautiful mysterious sound."; "left a Canada House audience haunted."

More expository comments have also been gifted, exampled by these:

> I have been fortunate enough to have conducted no less than three of Clement's works, on three separate occasions. Clement's music has within it the essential ingredient so craved by all composers; originality. To study a score of Clement's is to experience a masterclass in the formation of musical ideas into a unique whole.
>
> *Steven Lloyd-Gonzalez, conductor*

On the songs:

> I've been listening ... with fascination to all the wonderful sounds and textures in your songs—there's so much atmosphere, which suits Sarah's voice perfectly [Sarah Verney[11]]. A lot for the listener to absorb, and I shall enjoy continuing to listen. *The Last Invocation* is a stunning poem and setting. *He would send me running* ... portrays perfectly the natural range of excited, breathless speech. ... You are writing at a very deep level of poetic experience, and that makes the songs extremely intense.
>
> *Delyth Wilkinson, singer and psychotherapist.*

And singer Wendy Nieper, who has sung extensively in the new music world, remarked to me (on the occasion of my 70th birthday concert, in which she was singing) that with other contemporary music she has sung, once you have the notes

---

11   Who was singing on the recording Delyth was listening to.

learnt, there often isn't much of anything else to hear. She contrasted that with my songs, which on subsequent visits, she averred, reveal deeper musical interest and emotional content than perceived at the first: Very gratifying !

A small handful of commissions and composition prizes have come my way: a choral piece, a bass trombone concerto,[12] and a duo for guitar and percussion, were each commissioned; a brass quartet, a piece for bassoon ensemble and a wind quintet won prizes. Owing to being somewhat reclusive in character, I eventually decided to ignore most competitions, largely because I did not perceive the gifts of music to be appropriate within egoic materialistic competitiveness. Those competitions requiring age restrictions are anyway looking for unknown youthfulness, so the perceptive constrictions of the 'gatekeepers' noted above apply. But I'm definitively out of those anyway: too old !

I was asked once what makes my work original. I replied with something like this: The short answer is ´that which erupts´, whatever that may imply. The long answer is not really possible in words, because as Mendelssohn remarked, words are far less precise than music, and I refuse personal musical analysis: that is for academics and those without musical soul.

Curious how the movement of the word ´original´ from its

---

12    Unfortunately the trombonist who had commissioned it died in an accident. He was a dear friend. I did not want it performed by any other trombonist, so put it away.

meaning of origin, what came first out of nothing, to currently implying simply ´new´ or 'novel', implying a prior foundation against which the novelty is discerned, has actually in the context of artistic work completed a full circle, implying ´this work has origins no other has´. Or so I assert it is intended to be understood: the term is routinely overused.

Contra to the difficulties I have outlined, I believe my early blindedness to life[13] has proved not only to be first a handicap, but also to be now somewhat of an advantage, in that not having had orthodox musical expectations inserted into me early, I have been obliged to work it all out for myself. It may surprise readers to note that I have no memories of popular music in my early life—no favourite songs etc.: All I recall is the BBC Light Orchestra which my father listened to on the radio, and too many dirge-like hymns in church ! My amnesia is apparently not completely rescued.

Having entered the work and life of composing, I couldn't imagine not doing it—until the fear pandemic declared a halt in 2020, for complex situational and personal reasons: In the ominous fog blanketed over us I found it became too difficult to muster the necessary strongly sustained focus, requiring a deeper, more spiritual, journey into personal depths than does writing these words.

Perhaps improvisation is now sufficient, piping to trees in the peace and emotional quietude of a wood. And the process

---

13   See *On being a late starting composer*

of formal composition was getting slower, too, simultaneously because of the gradual slowing down of my advancing age, and because my perception and understanding of what *real* music *is* continues to expand, thus requiring ever more careful estimates of where the contemplated work *presently is.* And my compositions are never completely finished, they continue to change— every time I look at a score some better way in some detail or other presents itself . . .

For example I revised songs originally written and performed with piano, to be accompanied by string quartet. In that form they were professionally recorded with three of my four string quartets, the first of which is also a song sequence.[14]

That usage of strings recalls the Elizabethan composers' innovation: Using the smooth blending of consorts of viols to accompany song, a radical departure from continental practices of the time. The English long favoured the smoothness of sonority over the three part differentiations enacted on the continent under Catholic Church restrictions referring to the holy triad.

That is the period and place in music history I feel most affinity with, which intuitional attraction was confirmed and clarified by writer and teacher Gordon Strachan, who elaborated an astrological structure predicated on the historiography of Charles Carter, whereby the position of ones birth

---

14  Recorded on the disc *The Coming of Light* - Wendy Nieper singing with the Astaria String Quartet. See Appendix 2 and *Recording references*

chart read across a map of the centuries indicates ones favoured phases in history.[15] Certainly, doing the mapping, the late Tudor period was clearly pointed to as primary for me.

The next three chapters cogitate on aspects of the mysterious world of sound which bear on how composers structure their compositions around the chosen sounds, and so how do I. We start with the structures of Indian music, which have long much attracted me.

15   Strachan 2006 pp157-61

# Four

# Time or Space

## A note on modality & traditional Indian music

All are but parts of one stupendous whole. *Alexander Pope*

THIS IS A DISQUISITION on the primary use of modes in my composing work. Modes exist singularly and thus do not dovetail into each other as in the tonal system of modulating keys explored in European 'classical' music during the 17th to 19th centuries.

Some analytical description is needed here in order to satisfactorily cover the topic. Maybe I should note that only after first diving into composition work did I then later discover the Indian classical forms as fitting what I had already attempted to start: nothing new in this world !

Modes are a much older system than the tonal, deriving from Ancient Greece and elsewhere. Without going too much into technical descriptions, the classical modes are different sequences of intervals, mostly but not quite all, various sequences of whole- and semi-tones, which provide differing feeling characters as suited to various compositional intentions —happy or mournful, and so on.

As a way of picturing the differences, tracking octaves on linear sequences of the white notes only of the piano keyboard, starting at different notes, will show nearly all the modes, except those with some intervals greater than the one tone built in intervals on the piano (one tone plus a bit). Some modes are familiar: C to C is the 'major' scale, A to A is the 'minor', in the classical modulated tonal system. The rest are unfamiliar, some often used, some rarely.

How did I arrive at the use of modes for my composing?

From the outset I sought to situate my work in the contemporary world, in so far as that could match personal authenticity, as examined in the previous chapter. Surveying the territory, I found, as counter to classical tonalism, some atonal work, some quite extreme: for examples Carter, Boulez, Murail, various Scandinavians, and others.

I observed, on the one hand, that aural experience of atonal music accustomed the inner ear to it, and on the other, that that accustomization of the neural pathways seemed to have itself furthered the extremes of modernism, a feedback process which had resulted in the alienation of much of the listening public, perhaps too many for the health of music as socio-cultural phenomenon.

Which also bears on much of the reason why composers working in those times in more traditional forms were unacknowledged by the gatekeepers—occulted let us say. And there were many. I posted a query on the web enquiring who was composing in traditional styles, and not being noticed. I was inundated: dozens of responders wanted to know if I could help them to get performed, even assumed that I could. Alas, no, not my rôle, not in a position to do so.

However some welcome *rapprochement* between contemporary composers and the listening public nonetheless seemed to happen in the last few decades of the 20thC, both sides shifting ground towards a mutual accommodation. And I, as well as others, came to the view that extreme atonalism/ serialism was the end mark of an investigative enterprise that left the legacy of a set of useful compositional tools, one set only among other families of technique.

I was influenced not only by recognising the socio-cultural situation alluded to above, but quite strongly by the meaningful presence of that natural acoustic object, the major/minor triad, together with its historically attendant functional harmony. I felt that the diatonic system was not lightly to be entirely discarded, being not only an aspect of natural harmonics, but also a still living presence in the collective cultural psyche, even though no less a figure than Stravinsky wished to define it as history. And, secondly, the essentially hierarchical properties of triads appear to be naturally part of the structure of our human hearing processes.

Writing on this, Fred Lerdahl suggested that if what he called compositional grammars do not relate to the hierarchical forms of cognitive processes (listening grammars), structural aspects of the music so composed will be incomprehensible, his main example of that being Boulez's *Le Marteau sans Maître*,[1] arguing that Boulez's permutational forms are unrelated to the functionality of the brain.[2]

True enough apparently, but on the other hand how many listeners comprehend J.S. Bach's number plays by audition alone?  And of those who do not (most of us, I suspect), who actually feels any loss in the affects his music brings?

At the same time, though, I don't personally find Boulez's compositions attractive, in the formal meaning of that adverb.[3]

However, my overall style choice is modal, which lacks the sense of forward movement, of anticipation, central to the articulated time of functional harmony—the structure of "classical" music.  Instead it tends to generate a spatial articulation, even a sense of timelessness, which I connect with the type of psychophysical state mentioned above.  An appreciation of Indian classical music is associated with that, a strong influence which has found its way into my works as aspects of *rāg* forms.[4]

The attraction of *rāg*, a monodic and centrally improvisatory form, rests on an æsthetic response which at its best transports the listener out of the every day perception of time as a more or

---

[1]  *The hammer without a head.*

[2]  Lerdahl 1988

[3]  See Chapter 7 in this volume.

[4]  *Rāga* is an older form of the word, still familiar in recent times. Contemporary Indian languages are tending to drop the final vowel, a common type of linguistic development. Both forms are found in recent literature.

less variable flow or passage from the future into the past via the present moment—Henri Bergson's *durée*—into a state in which that flow is forgotten, and the 'moment' of the performance is extended immeasurably. The phrase 'out of time' captures the essence of it: *extempore* indeed.

How this is achieved by Indian musicians in performance is a matter of continuing investigation by several writers, particularly by analysis of time measurement. The term *lay* or *laya* arises here, and like other terms used in the long history of Indian music its meanings and significances have changed substantially through time. Some scholarly digging seems appropriate here.

Martin Clayton noted that it has been "appreciated that *lay* is partly responsible for the æsthetic character of music" citing the Visnudharamorttara Purānā (an encylopædic text) which correlates *lay* with *ras* (or *rasa*), another important concept, indicating the mood or emotional flavouring of the *rāg*, which perhaps lends credence to the idea of apparent timelessness noted above.[5] However he barely explores that, favouring attention to other meanings of the term, equating with pace, tempo, and rhythmic density, or as a general term for rhythm.

Effectively this is choosing the anatomising approach of western reductive thought, as also on the whole does Lewis

---

[5]   Clayton 2000 p75

Rowell,[6] though he does suggest that

> *laya* ... represents the phase of rest in the continuous
> alternation of action and repose which is the essence of the
> traditional concept of temporality in music ... one of the hall-
> marks of Indian thinking.[7]

Seemingly another hint.

Of those I have read on this subject only Philip Rawson
attempts to analyze the heard sense of long breathed phrasing
spanning across the boundaries of *rāg* rhythmic cycles (named
*tal*) which seems to be part of what determines the æsthetic
response noted above. He suggests that *laya*

> is closest to the sustained phrasing of fine string playing, eg
> Pablo Casals and Josef Szigeti [who were able] to generate
> time-shapes which are individually far longer than any tie-
> marking can notate, and can only be arrived at intuitively.[8]

This seems to me to bear meaningfully on the conundrum.
Perhaps it is the spanning across rhythmic boundaries which is
part of the intuitionally felt sensation of spatiality, in contrast to,
for example, a long held dominant heard as foretelling a resolution in classical European polyphonic music—the fifth yearning for closure at the final.

This topic deeply concerned my compositional endeavours.

---

[6]   Rowell 1992 p189 *passim*

[7]   *op.cit.* p202

[8]   Rawson 1996 p36

By incorporating borrowings from the Indian tradition into western music forms I aimed to import something of that out-of-time feeling, though 'hope' might have been a more appropriate term, as the possibility of success was highly debatable, probably in part owing to the fundamental disparity between monody and the prevailing polyphony/homophony.[9]

At the very least *rāg* forms are pitch set resources for the modal composer, and their referential properties—time of day of performance, intended mood—at least philosophically pleasing. Certainly this practice simultaneously loosened up and structurally defined my composing . . .

Next we have a look at the effects of linear proportionalities in the structures of music as experienced in heard time-spans.

---

[9] Technical terms for combinations of several parts, or for a single part with accompaniment.

# Five

## Sectio Aurea? Fibonacci? Who cares?[1]

*Our biggest failure is our failure to see patterns.* Marilyn Ferguson

A NUMBER OF COMPOSERS over the centuries have apparently been interested in utilising the proportions of the Sectio Aurea, aka the Golden Section (GS) or Golden Mean, Divine Proportion, or Greek letter Phi, mathematically cited as approximately 1/0.618.

Conservatoire students to whom I introduced a Chopin piece to illustrate this proportionality—somewhat surprising perhaps?—were utterly shocked that the prince of romantic pianists could possibly have structured a piece using rational mathematical thinking. Well, he did do an academic thesis on these proportionalities. Some details are at the chapter ending.

The proportion is also related to the Fibonacci sequence constructed to solve a problem relating to rabbit population by the 13th Century Italian mathematician Leonardo Bonacci, which 'happens' to approach and then meet the Golden Section (GS) proportion as the numbers increase: each number is the sum of the previous two. So 0, 1, 1, 2, 3, 5, 8, 13, 21, 34, 55 and so on.

Everything, without exception, is connected. These number plays define, and are felt as, proportions in the flow of music.

---

1  Slightly edited version of a note in the *Severnside Composers' Alliance Newsletter.*

In music the proportions are obviously linear.  The proportions are also found for example in Ancient Greek Architecture in the relative distancing of, particularly, rows of frontal columns, where the outer pair are fractionally closer to their neighbours than are the rest within the row.  They have also been long used to define the proportions of a space, with dimensions at right-angles, and also found in the opening out of spiral forms.

Why are they held to be important?  The answer is that they are innate to our beingness, the proportions occurring naturally everywhere, from spiral galaxies through human body proportions to snail shells and yet smaller, and in plant forms, as any perceptive gardener will notice, defining branching positions and directions of growth which particularly provide the maximum exposures to sunlight as the branching proceeds to spiral up the central growth.

In the human body, proportions include the relations of hand to forearm, head to spine to legs, and facial proportions. If these are present in exactitude in a human body, that person is likely perceived as truly beautiful.  In most of us they are approximate at various proportions, but still can be noticed. The Golden Section is also found embedded in the DNA spiral, at the centre of life's growth.

So it is at least possible to suggest that the pervasiveness of the proportions we are discussing, which are all around us, were very likely subliminally absorbed into our unconscious minds during ordinary development, whether or not we may later consciously note such things.

So when we create something—architecture, music—the subliminal proportionalities referring to the natural world including ourselves affect the work, perhaps coming out of our unconscious into our conscious mind, which is currently focussed on the creation of the piece we are envisaging. Therefore we naturally tend to build those proportionalities into the work, as do fellow creators. These actions are not necessarily wholly conscious, but nevertheless they provide a natural satisfaction, most certainly emotive, which we may then, having become aware of them, rationalise into well used formulas.

I have deliberately aimed at the GS in compositions, but not at all always, and where I have not, have sometimes in a sudden clarity noted that I have intuitively placed a climax pretty near the Golden Section point—two thirds through is not that far beyond. Though, with a careful and thoughtful survey, I then feel that a climax at the two thirds point means that the ending comes a mite too soon. A climax half way through is definitely too soon, too consciously rationalized.

How do we illustrate the Golden Section? Linearly, draw a line of 100 units (millimetres, or 16$^{ths}$ of an inch, 6¼ inches) and mark where 61.8 occurs—62 is near enough at these scales. A large sheet of paper will be required. In two dimensions, using compasses, draw an exact square of that size; draw a diagonal up across, treat that as a fulcrum and arc it from the foot to extend the side of the square where it ends. That is now the side of a larger square.

And there we have it, defining two dimensions as the extended horizontal and the vertical line. To draw a spiral (galaxies, snail shells) make a circular continuum of squares at Fibonacci rate, and so increase the curve size as you progress outward—as in this diagram.

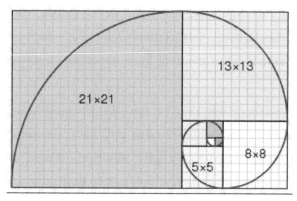

Or just consult the internet. Not so engaging though!

In the flow of music it follows from the notion of unconscious or subliminal creational factors that appreciation by recipients of the creation are also naturally governed by unconscious forces as well as conscious knowledge of fashions, cultural prevalences, and so on. Therefore it is not necessary to be cognisant of all the above in order to enjoy the music. Bach's number plays, invisible to most of us, I feel were mainly for his personal enjoyment.

Bartok is probably the commonest known in his use of the Golden Section, though how did he decide on positions for the change? I found a problem when considering this, owing to having to decide whether to count the measures (bars), or calculate elapsed time. The problem is particularly acute when pauses or metrical changes occur.

I think the less problematic answer is to adopt the elastic time formula, and so stick with what the audible rhythms support: that is to say, bar (measure) or beat counts, with calculated time changes included. After all, steadily passing time is just boring clock time, but time is immensely flexible in our real ordinary perceptions (Bergson's *durée* again), engaged activity shrinking the felt passing of time, and boredom stretching it (with a yawn).

We do need some examples. Golden Section or Fibonacci sequences have been enthusiastically identified in the work of many composers, but it may well be that in some, possibly many cases, the appearance in a work was more a matter of the unconscious than of deliberate planning by the composer, as noted above.

Nevertheless here is Beethoven seemingly on the mark with a motto in the first movement of his *Fifth Symphony*. The motto reoccurs after 377 measures, and again after another 233 measures. $233/377 = 0.618$. Also the coda is 129 measures, and after 49 bars a completely new tune starts: $49/80 = 0.6125$, only very slightly off ... Doesn't matter? But who knows ! How do we *feel*, while hearing the music?

We should include a Bartok example. The first movement of *Music for Strings, Percussion and Celesta* is 89 measures long: the climax appears at measure 55; $55/89 = 0.6179$, plenty close enough. On Fibonacci numbers, violin mutes begin to be removed at 34, then replaced at 69, notes the Hungarian scholar Ernö Lendvai, though what 69 is doing there out of the overall sequence I fail to see! A bit of practicality necessitated, maybe.

However, Chopin. My example is the *Prelude No.1 in C:* the 8th measure, lowest note (end of introduction); 13th, suggestion of key change; 21st, climax (*ff* marking); the piece ends at the 34$^{th}$ measure—8, 13, 21, 34. Which illustrates the 'pause' problem—how do you count it?: I discussed that difficulty with composer/pianist Geoffrey Poole. The answer seemed to be implied in the remark on Bartok's rhythms given above: go with the heard rhythms. And so here we have a Fibonacci sequence. Who can say whether that was conscious or unconscious. We may, though, allow that he placed the climax at the Golden Section position. Several other of his piano pieces also show such structural leanings.

Next, amp it up, calm it down: sharp, soft: harsh, smooth.

# Six

# How do we hear dissonance?[1]

*Music is a hidden arithmetic exercise of the soul.  G.W. Leibniz*

ALL MUSIC CONSISTS OF tension and release, the tension of dissonance released into consonance.  Without this bipolarity there is no music.  That's a bit bald, but I'll stick with it.  The Medieval Roman Church authorities claimed they were achieving a godly consonance by issuing compositional rules, three voices only to reflect the masculinised holy threesome.  Though their strictures were perhaps more to do with banishing the feminine, fear of the new, and countering equally feared defiance of authority, as ever was, and is !

The only true consonances are unison, and the octave.  The perfect fifth is next best, but listened to carefully with very open ears there is a slight *frisson* even there.  I refer to pure intervals, not the conveniently adjusted ones adapted to diatonic key changes which are already tuned on the modern piano ready for the player.  And there is a gradation of dissonance through the rest of the intervals.  Even our much loved third, held now to be beautifully consonant, was officially regarded as a dissonant interval for a couple of centuries after Léonin and Pérotin began experimenting with over-lapping lines of chant in 12/13thC France.  How our hearing evolves, if that's all that

---

1   Also a slightly edited note from the *Severnside Composers' Alliance Newsletter.*

happened. Given time we simply get used to sonic novelties. Our habits of hearing loosen: we grow into the changing sonic worlds..

The case of plainchant is instructive. It is a pattern of movement away from and back to consonance with the Final, the fundamental note of the mode. Without that note sounded as a drone, aural memory is needed to supply the pattern of tension and release with and from the Final. Memory itself does not need to be completely conscious to supply musical effect, though the result is subtly better if listeners and singers, and indeed all instrumentalists too, do have a clear sense of the Final in their minds.

I have my private suspicions (for which there is probably not an iota of evidence) that in the historic past, when European plainchant was less disconnected from its older world roots, it would have been chanted to a drone, and also set at an octave (or more?) lower than we are used to today, which would bring it into line with many other chant traditions around the world.

Recordings of Victorians speaking indicate that most of them were residing in their heads—speaking high in the head voice, whereas far more people in our day speak nearer to or in the chest voice, thus down in pitch, and so richer psycho-sociologically. Consequently when it came to resurrecting Gregorian chant the Victorians placed the tessitura high. One might comment here on materialistic intellectualism, fully manifesting during the 18th and 19th centuries, and so the increasing use of the head voice, we may consequently deduce. The phrase 'coming to a head' springs to mind.

But even the history of drone is unclear. The very long story of Indian musics suggests that the use of drones was a relatively late introduction, that chants were sung alone in earlier times. Does that imply that the hearing of the ancients was somehow finer than in more recent times? That may well be true, referencing our current noise polluted *soi disant* civilization where most of us have consequently, perhaps necessarily, lost the finer nuances of the hearing organism, the loss exampled by police and ambulance sirens set at levels able to penetrate vehicles' closed windows, simultaneously causing damage to unprotected ears.

Or was drone simply a brilliant invention?

Even so, the rise and fall of the sung line has always carried its dissonance and consonance messages, however attenuated the hearers' consciousness of it, and that is true of the heard profile of many musics. Similarly, in diatonic, and often un-avoidable in atonal music, a long held note will tend to take on the character of a pedal note approaching a cadence (something atonal composers have to beware of !), the fifth yearning for completion at its tonic. Which means it is not heard as a strict consonance with that tonic, sounding or not, but rather as integral to the entire bundle of sounds which are aurally defined by the held note as a diatonic key fifth.

So dissonance is an integral part of musics. What we use the word for changes through time, naturally, as music evolves, as do our aural experiences. Most of us now would not regard intervals of fifths, fourths and thirds as dissonant. And since the bold step taken by Wagner of treating the minor seventh chord as more than just a cadential device, but an engaging harmonic in its own right, we might consider *that* interval to be consonant too. Some of us used to hearing more recent musics might also declare that the interval of a major second, compared with the minor second, is consonant. Certainly a sequence of minor seconds followed by a major second has the feeling of release from tension.

It is all relative. Some of the oldest known European folk music, from the eastern edges of what is now Hungary, exhibits sequences of parallel major seconds. In some sense this could be the harmonic equivalent of the sharp biting vocal edges of traditional singing in parts of the Middle East, generating dissonant overtones. The gorgeously resonant Georgian male voice choir unexpectedly comes to mind, perhaps as contrast.

For musics specifically tailored for sonic healing therapy, the points made above still apply, even though the sound therapist may be consciously avoiding the sharper dissonances in circumstances which require as much consonance as possible, such as keeping a patient in unconsciousness for medical purposes, for which the musical sounds are aimed at providing subconscious healing resonances. On the other hand, as can happen in classical music therapy, when the client needs to express deep emotional distress, she or he may well instinctively create strongly dissonant music to 'amp up' the tension within in order to trigger the healing release.

As for the equal tempered scale and its unnatural though accepted compromised pitches, none the less these supply their own additions to the evident dissonances. Or do they, in all circumstances? Interestingly, it is apparent from studies done on singers that those hearing the live performance 'forgive', unconsciously, quite wide variations from ideal pitches in passing notes, in many cases much wider than the equal temperament compromises.

Similarly, in traditional Indian *rāg* performances, where each performer has his own tuning protocols, it is (maybe more 'it was' in view of modern communications) not uncommon to hear a familiar *rāg* with distorted intervals, perhaps stretched, widened a little, or diminished. But 'distorted' is the wrong word where the performer is sufficiently accomplished, for then the audience happily accepts the musicality of the performance, not finding the distorted intervals dissonant in themselves, but part and parcel of *that particular* performer's musical essence.

Not so in recordings, however, in the fixedness of which misspitches are notoriously noticeable. I feel the difference is that in live performances players and audience are connected in more than the sounds, they are also bound together (perhaps on the carrier waves of our bodily electromagnetism) in the emotional, or indeed even spiritual, ambience of the performance occasion. This is not, and probably cannot be, present with recordings listened to privately.

There is something here to do with the ways in which we are a social species, and parallel to the way the talking cure therapist picks up the otherwise hidden emotional state of the client.  There also appears to be somewhat less tolerance of pitch inequalities in, at the least, western instrumental playing. Primacy of the voice?  Or past the tolerance level of equal temperament tuning?  I leave that question to be cogitated on as you will.

So the answer to the question which sparked this writing, 'what is our reaction to dissonance?' is entirely context dependent.  I can, like many others, find the roar of city traffic intolerably dissonant when out in it.  But given some space away, perhaps inside an adjacent building where there is some attenuation, I can also hear it meditatively as part of the sounds of the 'city symphony', with its wide band background drone and foreground louder vehicles with different pitch engine noises sounding the Doppler effect as they pass, accompanied or punctuated by hootings of various pitches, the grumbling sounds of rubber on the tarmac, and maybe in a slight lull in the traffic, the sounds of people walking, and birds flying past.

Take it away for yourself !

I knew someone once, who declared in tones of authority that 'there is no dissonance in Bach'. His belief was that music 'stopped' there. Anyone with a modicum of musicality knows that Johann Sebastian's music is absolutely rife with major seconds, expressed also as minor sevenths and major ninths, and not a few minor seconds and derivatives too, all part of the to-and-fro rhythms of tension and relaxation which are the lifeblood of music. That same person complained loudly that 'the rot started with Beethoven!' he hearing nothing but 'noise'. I shall not name him. Quite rare, maybe, such a strong fixation on historical period musical definitions and practices.

Whether and how we hear dissonance or not is also instru-ment dependent. Complex chords played on a harpsichord prior to a resolution sound far less discordant than the same chords played on a modern piano, as witness the astonishingly modernistic one-chord-on-top-of-another in the harpsichord music of J.S. Bach's exact contemporary Domenico Scarlatti. The heard difference is in the considerably greater prominence of overtones on the piano (with a nod in the direction of baroque tunings, differing somewhat from the modern so called 'equal' tunings).

And here we might note that the natural harmonic overtone

sequence itself produces its own dissonances against the fundamental note, from the seventh upwards, at first the odd numbered harmonics.  Interestingly, however, they do not sound particularly dissonant (to my contemporary ears) at their natural pitch distances from the fundamental:  for example the seventh harmonic is two octaves and a flattened minor seventh from the fundamental.  Put them both into the same octave, and they do plainly sound dissonant.  So here is another context to make note of in this discourse—octave separation eases the apparent dissonance.

Rudolf Steiner related the intervals in an octave to consciousness, delineating the journey from internality to engagement externally.  This seems a good way to finish this little discussion.  I am indebted to music therapist and wise-woman Sarah Verney for what follows, for she put it together as shown below.

Single tone:    Absolute rest. Inner experience

Minor second:  Something begins to move. Still an inner activity or movement, remaining within the self.

Major second    Activity increases. Carries inner movement further. Disturbance wishes to find rest.

Minor third:    Experience of inner balance. Still an inner experience, leaning back to the second, from whence it came.

| | |
|---|---|
| Major third: | No longer leans back. An important statement of inner balance. Positive. An expression of inner self. "Music comes from within". |
| Perfect fourth: | Inner movement, but reaching towards the outside. Taking a first step towards the outer relationship. |
| Augmented fourth (tritone): | Possibility of choice. Could withdraw or take a step to the fifth. Courage required to face an outer experience with which one can relate. |
| Fifth: | Putting out a hand. Facing an outer experience. |
| Minor/major sixth: | Both continuing to move out. The major sixth is a still greater step outwards. |
| Minor seventh: | Tension between oneself and the outside world. |
| Major seventh: | The height of being outside the self. Tension reaches its highest point. |
| Octave: | The ego is caught in relation to outer experience. Fulfilment. |

# Seven

# What price another Way?

## Musings on life and music at the death of Boulez.[1]

### A SENSE OF HISTORY

UNLESS WE KNOW OUR HISTORY, where we have come from, physically, emotionally and spiritually, we do not completely know who or what we are. This remark may be supported by noticing the many people who seem lost in this world. Yes, we are in an unwinding culture: that is certainly true. I am suggesting here a small relief from the sense of despair which too easily arises, as better than blindly denying that there is anything wrong, consciously or not: being aware of our pasts, individual and collective.

I know, for instance, that my surname is cognate with Jules, Julian, Jolyon, Jill, Gillian, and the like, all derived from the Roman name Julianus, from Julius, as with the Emperor Julian. This suggests that my family name very likely has been in these lands since the Romans were in England, by whatever spelling: numerically most Jewitt's are still found concentrated around and within Newcastle, in the North-East of England, despite much movement south through the centuries since, which hist-

---

[1]   Based on a paper presented to a symposium at Bristol Music Club, Oct. 2016, on the legacy of Pierre Boulez, who had died earlier that year.

oricity discernibly supports immigrant origins in the construction and manning of the Roman Wall—on this argument my ancestor was a Roman soldier, or one of the supporting accompaniers.

This gives me a sense of belonging far greater than the simple knowledge that I was born here, here being the living landscape of what is now called England. That is my personal backdrop, shared with many others, which naturally infuses everything I do or think about, consciously or not.

On music, in parallel fashion, what I feel sure about is that this cannot have any meaning beyond the abstractly conceptual if it is not also rooted internally, where there is resonance with sensed reality. This is for me fundamentally important, no less in music than all else: feet firmly on the ground, feelings and thoughts thoroughly connected with that which intuition supported by thinking defines as authentic.

My philosophical outlook is situated with the phenomenalists, Husserl, Merleau-Ponty, David Abram. From this arises a desire to aim compositional work towards an encouragement of a psycho-physical state which is a grounded place of peaceableness, freedom from existential fears, which at its best can last well beyond the place and time of hearing, unlike the *ersatz* 'highs' commonly preferred—thus I suffered the fate of the nonconformist ! At least 'we' are not killed in recent times, contra historic ways of dealing with the disagreeing. We are merely 'deleted': merely?

And so in my personal search for authenticity in composition, I needed to find my own individual way into the labyrinth of modernisms, making my own choices of techniques and styles to investigate and use. Nothing unusual there, we might say . . .

I am not antagonistic to formally serialist music: I have used some of the techniques myself, together with other ways of writing. However, in Boulez' 'total serialism' works he seems to me to have completely boxed himself into purely intellectual processes. A perspectival view suggests his trajectory was an interesting endeavour (following Messiaen), perhaps even a necessary step in the progress of the crisis of renewal of Western music following the dying off of the old diatonic system. It is part of the strength of the man that he did publicly admit that most of those works were "satisfying mental exercises, nothing more."

This maybe indicates my rather odd personal parallel with Boulez: making rules and finding the need, or sometimes reasons, to break them. Indeed experiencing the hard intellectualism of computer software designing in my previous career was what enabled me to perceive that much *more* was required in creating music. And I often prescribe myself compositional limiting rules in order to facilitate coherence in the work—*those* rules are not for breaking ! I will not present any detail here.

Likewise, and more collectively, I need to know and under-stand how we in Western culture got to where we are, the diatonic system of three centuries having played itself out. Where do we go from here? Was Boulez' answer the best one? I want to track back and observe.

If not Boulez, would someone else have come forward to declare the One Answer? Why did second generation French modernists (Les Six) put Debussy into the cultural background, temporally at least, or indeed why did the sons of J.S. Bach consider their father 'old fashioned' in their times. Same answer: the fickle attraction of the new, the novel—just like now, so also then!

And why was the English musical renaissance of the early 20thC a near miss? Partly, or maybe largely, owing to the deter-mined critical hostility at that time denigrating the English in favour of preferential German music as the only music deserv-ing of acclaim.

A fleeting thought. How *much* was Boulez' energetic trajec-tory an aspect of historic Franco-Germanic rivalry, however much disguised, however much not noticed? The cultural dissonances here can perhaps be perceived in the contrasts between the lads' night out in Bavarian bierkellers, singing simple ditties, and the finely differentiated nuances in Moulin Rouge presentations, which says nothing about intelligence as such: for all psychologies are founded on culture as well as physicalities and personal energy variations, which are also in turn collectively founded on geography. The sense of place rears its head again.

❖　　❖　　❖　　❖　　❖

## CULTURE: THE SHRINKAGE OF GEOGRAPHY

Do we understand how we are situated in the world? The 20<sup>th</sup>C saw vast changes in common understandings and so outlook, particularly in the Western loosely labelled civilisation: Two world wars with an economic disaster between, burgeoning international travel and the growth of the internet and related technical developments—all massively contributed.

In this period we have seen the category of World Music defined, with consequent crossovers of, for example, Western classical and popular Indian with jazz, and we hear elements of classical in pop, and pop in classical, as well as much other borrowing. I have myself used Indian *Rag* forms as, at the least, templates.[2]

Such usages speak, in a sense, to the reversal, the boustrophedon, the ox turning, of historic separations, an old example of which is the separation of poetry texts from their traditional ancient musical element, vocal connectivities in the form of singing, this movement allowing space for purely instrumental music to appear in the 14<sup>th</sup>C, and poetry to lose its

---

[2]　See Ch. 4

complete ancient association with the sung line.

In terms of location linked to culture, we can understand why somewhat isolated England persisted in not following continental musical leadings, and then twice provided the dominant voice: Dunstable and the English *discant*, and later, the Elizabethans teaching the continentals about sonority as an alternative to the habit of three voice highly differentiated lines —ruling Roman Catholicism declaring anathema on anything else.

We can understand why classical music becomes *other* in places far from the central hub of Europe: for example Malcolm Williamson creating music to my ear evincing the wide spatial geography of Australia: he lived and worked in Britain, but he grew up, and therefore formed early perceptions, reactions and attitudes, in his native Australia.

Maxwell Davies, who died in the same year as Boulez, requires a mention as a rather different composer. Max, we can agree I think, reacted in his music to the stark treeless country-and-sea-shore panorama of his adopted home in Orkney.[3]

All of these and other understandings are situated within and flow from our personal internal resonances with the world *out there*, a world which we feed with what we do and be, and which reciprocally feeds us: These connectivities are expressed

---

[3]  Orkney, it is said, experiences nine months winter and three months bad weather !

through direct experience mediated by our understandings and knowledge. And this is itself irremovable from our culture, with due deference to individual perceptions, inventions, inner growth, orientations: what we individually are able to accept, and give.

With all that in mind, in my view it is simply not possible, in any endeavour, to sweep away the past in the belief that something radically new can be inserted into the vacuum—*there never is a cultural vacuum, it cannot be created*. That in a nutshell is my objection to Boulez' enterprise: he left out, or attempted to leave out, the very human dimensions which I have attempted to outline above and elsewhere. Revolutionaries of all stripes have always set out to demolish the culture they find wanting. The trouble is, to rework Einstein's remark, you cannot create the new with the mindset which demolishes the old. Which old mindset is inevitably what revolutionaries work with, instead of first dealing with their own inner demons.

Well, this presentation has said nothing much about how Boulez actually composed. I intended from the start to consider more philosophical attitudes, and how that throws light on the subject of Pierre Boulez' extraordinary life and wilful project to banish European music's entire past in favour of a limited conception of what so called classical music could be 'permitted' to advance into. I trust that the somewhat fragmental discourse above shows something of how impossible such a project was bound to be.

Which is not at all to dismiss the man and his work. He left a body of fine modernist compositions, if mostly too abstract for my feeling comprehension, and some worthy of forgetting, much like the output of all composers, including myself. And, perhaps more memorably, a collection of splendidly illuminating conducted recordings.   Both those work results will endure.


## POSTSCRIPT

Rudolf steiner, working from his focus on mankind's evolution and the different stages of that which are geographically apparent within his vision, considered that the English were or would be faced with 'transformations' in which, in the words of Walter Johannes Stein, his follower, "feelings, hitherto unknown, will evolve. And it is at this point that we must expect a new phase of English music."[4]

I leave it there, passing on to the compositional outlook of another contemporary composer.

---

[4]  *English Music.* IN Steiner followers 1951 p72

# Eight

## "In Quest of Spirit: Thoughts on Music."

> When the words come, they are merely empty shells
> without the music. They live as they are sung, for the
> words are the body and the music the spirit.
>
> *Hildegard of Bingen*[1]

THE BOOK WITH THE TITLE REUSED HERE, by renowned composer Jonathan Harvey, is about music as mediator, a mysterious bridge connecting the mundane world to that other realm, which requires, whatever level of comprehension is possible for us incorporated beings, not only the grasp of intellect, the Western way, but also the way of Eastern mystics, contemplation, a sense of 'allowing', intuition we may call it, as knowledge in the sense of an immediate apprehension. In short, the realm of spirit.

This chapter is a review of Harvey's book, compiled because I was thoroughly smitten by what Jonathan had written, bearing on matters concerning human life on this planet viewed through the lens of music and music making,[2] precisely what *this* book endeavours to elucidate.

And music *is* mysterious. Subjectively, few people would doubt that music conveys meaning, communicates *something*. But what? Literary or visual art critiques are readily under-

---

1  Head quote inserted for the current book
2  Harvey 1999. Reviewed for Music & Psyche Journal, Feb 2003

standable by informed readers.  Discourse on music, on the other hand, is either technical, thus alienating those who are not musically trained, or tending towards the fancifully descriptive, thus tending to alienate those who are.  Harvey's book seeks to avoid those extremes, leaning gently into necessary technicalities.  Music does not accommodate itself to verbal description: it exists in another dimension.

Jonathan Harvey, one of the most respected of modern English composers,[3] asks 'Who is the composer?'  And, asserting from the start that music by its nature is associated with at least a latent spirituality, seeks to elucidate whose 'voice' is therefore speaking in the music.  Is meaning a fixed attribute of the musical sounds themselves, or is it a function of the listener's response?  The composer, whether as a human individuality or as the vessel for transmission of the music from *somewhere else* (there may in the end be no real distinction), is sometimes at the centre, sometimes at the periphery of events in the unfolding sounds.  And it is part of Harvey's purpose to attempt to show how these and other dichotomies are transcended by virtue of the spiritual connection music has, noticeable potentially if not always actually.

The route to his conclusions leads through considerations of the role of ambiguity, the concept of unity as transcendence of duality, and of the role of stasis and silence in music, the art of

---

3  Died in Dec 2012

movement through time.

The central role of ambiguity in Western polyphonic music is illustrated by Harvey with, among other examples, the opening of Mahler's 9th Symphony, where the opening bare notes 'A', apparently the centre of the new musical universe, are displaced in turn by harp, horn and beyond, introducing new notes and rhythms which cause the listener to revise understanding of the first hearing. The 'A' becomes the periphery.

Such movements Harvey likens to the ebb and flow of ordinary life. Just as the task there may be seen as a striving for unity, a bringing together of disparate personality attributes (Jung's individuation process) so he notes:

> A quintessential theme in music history ... at least up to Boulez and Birtwistle, has been that the greater the contrasts successfully unified in a single work, the more important that work seems to be.

That leads on to the consideration of unity, its meaning in discussion of the world of spirit as much as in that of music. Once we have perceived the limits and constrictions of verbal language, we may more readily apprehend the truth that unity in the spirit, the province of the contemplative, who *knows* by emptying the mind, is reported in the perennial mystical traditions as essentially indescribable: 'unity' being the one word most commonly used as signifier, a convenient label for that which is beyond verbal description.

In music unity may be in underlying structure; in an absence of discourse; or in stasis: a long held chord or note, or silence. Spirituality in music seems more apparent the greater the contrasts which have been unified, stasis or silence in particular tending to invite the spiritual to appear: He notes "the exposure of spirit when the discourse dies down". And

> Stillness permeates energy. Energy is shot through with stillness. In tantric Buddhism … this power is related to the union of emptiness and bliss.

The last chapter of Harvey's book discusses stasis and silence in music in the context of the two forms of possible transcendent experience: First, psychologist Abraham Maslow's 'peak experience', an unpredictable and generally sudden opening up of perception to an apparent, and radiant, other realm. And on the other hand, to become intentionally silent and still in the process of meditation, which may lead through years of practice to a profound state of 'emptiness' nevertheless pregnant with limitless possibilities: "It is said to be the womb of all creativity."

He reaches his conclusion, via several musical examples at the end of the book, that music exists beyond the subject/object duality:

> It still needs us to lend a willing ear, but if the process works, it transcends the subjective, it even transcends our "core," just as it transcends duality, and we can say—as we can say that

we and the music are one—that music is by its very nature spiritual or that we and the music are spiritual. Fundamentally, and following tradition, the "spiritual" is the experience of unity.

All turbulence, all suffering, arises from erroneously imputing real (as opposed to conventional) existence to "I" and "the other". When this is deeply understood … compassion is felt. Seeing through suffering … is "compassionate wisdom". Music is a picture of "wisdom". That is why music of suffering is often, paradoxically, so beautiful … Who then, in the last analysis, is the composer? The composer has no inherent existence. All one can say is that the "composer" is focussed towards wisdom, inseparable from the universe: the universe is expressing itself.

These can seem startling pronouncements. It is therefore legitimate to ask whether the preceding discourse sufficiently supports them. The grand themes tackled in the attempt to elucidate music's connection with the world of spirit, whether music has meaning, and if so what meaning, and therefore how does the composer actually relate to the texts produced, these have been, and no doubt will be again, examined in greater detail than is possible within the small compass of this book. Philosophers of music such as Edward Cone (*The Composer's Voice*) or Peter Kivy (*The Corded Shell and several other titles*), which examine the paradoxes of musical description, or Victor Zuckerkandl (*Sound and Symbol. Vol.2. Man the Musician*) have noted with care the areas of uncertainty in objective knowing which are embedded in their (and likewise Harvey's) themes.

Has our author over-generalized, then? The academic, objective view of his text would be that he has. However, the origin and purpose of his book throws light on this difficulty, if it is a difficulty. It began life as the 1995 Ernst Bloch Lectures at the University of California, a lecture series which brings distinguished figures in music to the Berkeley campus from time to time. Harvey comments::

> These lectures, given to a non-specialist public … were an attempt to address a subject fairly objectively and musico-logically. I was subsequently persuaded that, while trans-forming them into a book, I should … make them more personal, unashamedly my own subjective viewpoint … An important reason for adopting this approach was the apparent impossibility … of giving definitive answers in a field such as the spirituality of music, probably even for a professional philosopher or theologian. Therefore I rewrote the book as one person's viewpoint.

The result is a text which moves at will between the epis-temological, concerning ways of knowing, and the ontological, concerning ways of being. This results occasionally in an apparent air that *something* is left unfinished, but nevertheless seems to have a certain logic in a book which seeks to explore the transcendence of dualities,[4] and which is essentially a

---

4   CG Jung's transcendent function, bridging the duality of opposites.

personal statement about the author's determined integration of his composing with his personal spiritual practices, rooted in the Catholicism he grew up in and a more recent allegiance to Mahayana Buddhism.

As such the book can be read, reflected on, or disagreed with by anyone concerned with the life of the spirit, whether or no Harvey's music is resonated with, whether or no the reader is technically trained in music.

Those who are not need not be dismayed by the extensive references to the exampled scores: for the most part recordings of those are readily obtainable, and as with the samples on the accompanying CD, the author guides the reader through. For the musically trained, composers or musicologists, and indeed performers, this book is also a valuable analytic and also an interpretive guide to Jonathan Harvey's own music, the choice of the music of others also elucidating his own compositional influences.

The bedrock on which this book and his composing is founded the author himself defines:

> I cannot conceive of spending my life in a heedlessly unethical pursuit. Composing is a part of trying to live a life "skillfully", as Buddhists say. One can compose from many different levels of the soul, base or elevated; the decision is important. ... I aspire to a future in which the deepest level of personality known to human beings, the radiant still point beyond words, is encouraged by music to become manifest.

What more could a composer aspire to?  Ultimately, beyond the flaws of language, certainly beyond any personal, subjective judgement of his music, and read with the same deep engagement that is presented within as required for we and the music to be one, I find this little book moving, and inspiring.

Nine

# Participative Spiritual Inquiry and the Music & Psyche enterprise[1]

THIS CHAPTER AIMS TO ILLUSTRATE the commonalities of two different modalities of co-operative action, open to all comers, each leading to similar experiences of interconnection at a deep personal, spiritual level.

The Common Ground Report, of a week long gathering initiated by Joycelin Dawes, entitled *Participative Spiritual Inquiry*, proposes that this experiential method may represent a possible way for people to work together in equality in a future beyond our present collapsing so-called civilization, centred as it is on individualistic self-seeking, competition and greed.

The *Music and Psyche* network (commonly known to its members as *M&P*) was created to encourage similarly meaningful interpersonal interactions within musical improvisation groups, also with a focus on spiritual aspects and the equality of individuals. The group was developed jointly by Sarah Verney, music therapist, Rod Paton, academic and improviser, Susan Nares, musician and therapist, Maxwell Steer, composer

---

1   A shorter version of this article appeared in the Scientific & Medical *Network Review* (now *Paradigm Explorer*) 99, spring 2009, pp9-11.  The Common Ground Reports quoted here appeared in *Network Review* 98: p24-27.  Here reviewed and edited.

and initiator of the Music & Psyche project, and myself.

The meaningfulness of these interpersonal developments is indicated by this comment on great art by Heidegger:

> the artist remains inconsequential as compared with the work, almost like a passageway that destroys itself in the creative process for the work to emerge.[2]

Substitute 'individual' for 'artist' and we have a concise description of the developing groups, in which 'inconsequential' is comparative, not pejorative, which distinction serves to point up the essential dignity of the truly autonomous individual.

However, the differences between these two communal activities need to be drawn out a little here.

❖   ❖   ❖   ❖   ❖

## PARTICIPATIVE SPIRITUAL INQUIRY

JOYCELIN DAWES' WEEK LONG Participative Spiritual Inquiry event desired to create "deeper levels of knowing and community" which can be built on in subsequent inquiries, with the purpose of generating working structures for a future greater co-operative society. More precisely the enterprise was seen as the first stage in a process aimed at creating equal membership groups able to perform tasks (potentially of any kind) without leadership, without inequalities felt or actual, and with the

---

2   As paralleled in Chapter 8 on Jonathan Harvey's thoughts.

sense that all members were co-operating without egoically competing, each utilising their best skills willingly, and all feeling easy and satisfied with outcomes—a move away from long habituated governor/governed polarities.

Dawes notes that what has been achieved so far

> is only an initial phase, not the end point. If participative inquiry is really to demonstrate how groups can work collaboratively, from a transpersonal and shared field of experience, this has to be grounded and anchored.[3]

This envisions a future we can only strive towards—most of us, perhaps especially in Western 'civilization', are not very near that ideal. It is a profoundly different aim from the usual developments of groups, which start with a target, usually formed by egoically determined leaders who know only what they wish or dream for, and will therefore readily, sometimes blindly, put down unready, dissenting or criticising followers.

The Common Ground Report itself is thoroughly participative, consisting of comments, observations and reflections on the experience given by participants. Those who participated had self decided to answer published invitations.

## MUSIC & PSYCHE

ON READING THE COMMON GROUND REPORT I was struck by the

3   S&M Network Review 98 p23

resemblance of several comments to certain outcome experiences of the particular approach to group musical improvisation developed by the Music & Psyche enterprise.

Our intentions, not as wide as the expected further development in Participative Spiritual Inquiry, were a desire to find a
musical experience in improvisation which touched transcendent realms, to generate an authentic experience of music
making in the middle of a spectrum of group interactions
ranging from the thoroughly therapeutic to the more or less
impersonally musical, thus opening to wider complementary
human attributes and experiences.

This intention formed slowly into clearer theoretical description through the process of building the process. At the
start our intentions were expressed solely through musical
practices, more intuitional than verbal. In the working out of
the group's way our practice became a method of informal
participative investigation, as well as a pleasurably meaningful
activity in itself.

Thus our end point was equivalent to Participative Spiritual
Inquiries "initial phase" and had no further ambitions, though
we did find that, in our rare business meetings, an initiatory
improvisation created harmony and respect in the ensuing
verbal discussions. I venture to claim, though, that 'common
ground' is reached more readily with music, because words can
be and commonly are used to hide behind, whereas music

cannot be, because it is non-verbal: there is no deceit possible—even deliberate musical 'borrowings' simply find their place in the new construction, acquiring a different musical 'meaning'; they cannot be heard as the original musical message, but just as a quotation if recognized.

❖     ❖     ❖     ❖     ❖

## THE NATURE OF MUSICAL IMPROVISATION

MUSICIANS OF VARIOUS SKILLS AND PROCLIVITIES tend to come together for joint music making focussed solely on the music as organized sounds to be projected at audiences. Most such musicians come to practices and performances with little thought of the way in which musical sounds (indeed all sounds) are capable of mediating profound changes to psyche and soma—the rather mis-called 'Mozart effect' is pertinent: temporarily enlarged perceptual and reasoning intelligence.[4]

I have taken part in improvising groups exhibiting this impersonality, and find them lacking at some deep level of experience, however satisfactory the music becomes *qua* music, compared to improvising with the Music & Psyche group.

However it is probably safe to say that, among other traditions, jazz musicians tend to be rather more aware of psychic effects, and to be fair to the so-called 'classical' music world,

---

4   Rauscher et.al. 1993:  Mozart's music is not alone in sparking the effect.

which I inhabit myself, there are signs among some practitioners of a conscious awareness of deeper affects.

One such is the North American musician Pauline Oliveros, pioneer of a more holistic view of what it is to be a musician, who has clearly critiqued the impersonality discussed here:

> The study of music needs to include the inner development of musicians as well as the acquisition of skills and theories. When I was a student of French Horn playing I was encouraged to play long tones in order to develop my embouchure. The reason given was excellent, but my instruction also could have included ways of listening and observing my own psycho-physical responses to the long tones I practiced. I could have been guided to notice how my breathing effected physical and mental changes, how different tones resonated in me and in the surrounding environment, however subtle the results might have been. Such observations might have served to encourage my inner development ... I could have been responding to guidance that included a dedication to the intention of sounding for well-being as well as for purely musical purposes. I could have been encouraged to see how my desire to be a musician could have a larger meaning and purpose than solely the attainment of skill.[5]

A resounding endorsement of the attitude supported in this writing.

Here I give a brief elucidation of the essentially non-verbal

---

5  Oliveros 1990: p.viii

interactions occurring within improvising groups.[6] Suffice to say that various modalities of sensing are employed, and the absence of words tends in my perception to shift consciousness to more holistic regions, at least in part, where there is more balance between activities in the brain hemispheres. Wider psychological studies of musicians generally find more balanced masculine and feminine qualities in both genders.

Improvisation has its own idiosyncratic formalities which are divergent from playing from pre-written scores, not least with regard to preparation before playing, at a personal and interpersonal level.

Experienced performance improviser Tim Hodgkinson reports spending time, with his partner Ken Hyder, in silence and darkness before performing in order to empty their minds of everyday trivia, then heightening their non-visual senses by moving around in the dark around each other, putting chairs in each others way and similar strategies to effect disorientation and sharpen responses, which are then taken on stage with benefit to the work.[7] Other performance improvisers choose to share their preparatory silence with their audience, to aid attunement.[8]

---

6  See Chapter 11 in this volume for a more comprehensive survey.

7  Hodgkinson 1996 p61

8  Scheiby 1995 p200

Not only the interpersonal preparation, but also interactions during improvised playing, as noted by Rod Paton,

> suggests the existence of an improvisational state—a continuum of *not knowing*, abandoning the certainty of prescribed form and entering into a period of transitional form where participants become only partly conscious of what is happening".[9]

Common Ground Reports note this:

> 'The sense of keeping going through a time of not knowing.'
>
> 'Our dark not-knowing.'

During three day M&P core group only meetings (perhaps intentionally working on the development of the process, but always for our pleasure), we habitually banished spoken word interactions for a period of perhaps 24 hours, in order to heighten (or deepen) musical encounters during and after that period, but also to prepare to be open to transpersonal dimensions. When such work gels in this way the group achieves a correlative "intense comradeship, in which [ordinary] distinctions disappear or become irrelevant",[10] a collective experience of the reality of the numinous.

This rather wonderful outcome was also reached in the best of the general meetings open to anyone attracted. And many were.

---

9 Paton 2001 p15—his emphasis
10 Ruud 1995 *IN* Kenny 1995

Music & Psyche participants comment:

> 'I'm suddenly filled with that joyous feeling again, and have a big smile on my face ! I have changed, and the world has changed.'

> 'I am different and it all feels different. I/we have to learn how to fit in differently.'

> 'Thank you for an amazing and deeply moving weekend, a new reality indeed.'

These feelings were echoed in the Common Ground Report:

> 'Collectively, we surrendered the rational through a painful and frustrating struggle through which we found a place beyond where knowing was replaced by meaning. There is a great sense of love and joy.'

> 'When I stopped trying to make this event into the 'head' experience that I had been expecting and instead went with the group's flow, I then got from it instead a heart experience—a powerful feeling, which has also stayed with me so far since, of love for the group, for my life and for life, and a gratefulness that all is very well.'

Here we see that 'intense comradeship', which exhibits affinities with the central period of transition in cultural rites of passage: "This is a situation marked by rolelessness, ambiguity, and perceived danger", against the pressures of which the participants develop the 'intense comradeship'.[11]

---

11 *op cit*

A similar situation occurs in the routine processes of intentional temporary community building as presented by M. Scott Peck.  He describes the beginning stage as "Pseudocommunity", when participants are striving self consciously to be 'nice', paralleled in the inexperienced improvising group by the stronger egos attempting to impose musical order on unready others, strategies in both situations to get things going instead of patiently allowing the group feeling, or ethos, to emerge.  A Common Ground Reporter describes it precisely:

> 'I got exasperated by what I perceived as middle class politeness and little peer accountability holding up the group's progress, but this turned out, I think, to be useful.'

Scott Peck considered it an inevitable, possibly necessary, stage, the first of the sequence which he describes, followed by:

> The misguided attempts to heal or lead in Pseudocommunity then break down into Chaos, where participants attempt to convert each other to their own treasured beliefs.  The only meaningful way out of that is—the crucial stage—Emptiness, where participants needfully, and painfully, reflect on their own "barriers to communication".[12]

The success of this, however difficult, calms all down in the real Community, all respectfully listening to, and hearing, each other in autonomous individuality:  the Common Ground and Music and Psyche now each operating successfully.

---

12    Scott Peck 1993

❖ ❖ ❖ ❖ ❖

## INTEGRAL FEELINGS & THE BEAUTY OF THE MOMENT

COMMENTS ON SUCH EXPERIENCES IN Music & Psyche events illustrate outcomes at an individual level. These were spontaneous comments mostly, sent by e-mail or greeting cards after the event. The Common Ground Report more carefully thought out texts, intended as Report contributions, illuminate the parallel.

Common Ground Report:

> 'The quiet joy and feeling of peace I experienced when we had come through the tangle of muddle, separation and darkness, into a clear space of underlying union, was indescribably beautiful. I felt the relief of knowing that staying with what happens in the moment, however difficult, leads to clarity and vision.'

Music & Psyche:

> 'Wow!! What an experience. I am processing away like crazy and reflecting back with my wife the events over the weekend. I have never felt so suffused by the Spirit as I do now, after all that has happened. How wonderful to spend such an uplifting and enlightening time in the presence of fellow travellers. All were my teachers.'

> 'It was a great privilege to share the dance with such beautiful people.'

Common Ground Report:

> 'It was a great privilege to do this journey with you all and I so
> much look forward to seeing you again.'

> 'I don't think it is too much to say 'heaven arose'. I could analyse
> it further; I could deconstruct it, but *I choose not to*. Its precious-
> ness is in my recollection of its integrity as an experience.'
> (emphasis added).

Early M&P events were nearly always recorded, but we
noted that, mysteriously, possibly inevitably, the most profound
sessions failed to be recorded:  We had forgotten to turn the
machine on after a break, or had not noticed that the recording
disk or tape was full. So now we *choose not to* record, perceiving
that the true meaning of the work resides not in any preser-
vation of the musical result, but in the feelings at the sounding
moment, carried out into 'ordinary' life.

Music & Psyche:

> 'There was a moment of real contact between myself and one of
> the other group members through the improvisation that moved
> us directly into the Transpersonal, which has stayed with me.'

Common Ground:

> 'What did I learn? - When to speak and when to remain silent
> *[this is also an important factor in improvisations: substitute 'play' for
> 'speak'. CJ]* To trust that the group has an intelligence of its own.
> To participate in an alchemical process of transformation.'

Mention of alchemy suggests one of Music & Psyche's not

infrequently defined themes for improvisation meetings, which seems appropriate to elaborate on here. This one was on dreams. Participants offered dreams which we then attempted to *feel into* musically. After a few of those I presented a development of an idea by colleague Rod Paton, and facilitated an improvisation based on a simple version of the Alchemical sequence, expressed as felt travel through a night into day: First, the Dark of night standing for the *Nigredo*, the *prima materia* on which the alchemist works; Secondly the *Albedo*, the first glimmerings of light; Thirdly the *Citrinitas*, the coming of dawn; and then the *Rubedo*, the full resplendent light of the sun, the successful culmination of the work.

One of the participants wrote it up:

> Clement then took the theme of dreams into a new realm by introducing a process for taking dream images to provide a structure for an improvisation. He asked us to take one image from a dream and draw it *[or write it, and, importantly, noting the associated emotion/feeling: CJ]*. We then each talked about it. From what we said Clement linked it to a particular stage of an Alchemical sequence related to psychic processes. Luckily we had dream images that corresponded to all the four stages *[almost inevitable in my experience! CJ]* and so four groups for the improvisation were formed.
>
> Each group in turn according to the stages of the alchemical process improvised between themselves using the feelings of their dream images as a source of inspiration in playing and

listening to each other.  All the other groups coloured and supported the themes that were emerging.  What was fascinating to see was how a point would come when the process of the improvisation was needing to move on into the next stage and a new theme would take shape led by that group.  Having started with the repetitive theme of a leaden thump of beating drums [the Nigredo! CJ], the improvisation moved through different moods to end in an energetic joyful climax.  The whole piece had an amazing amount of energy in it and was distinctly different in quality from the earlier free improvisations.

These matters were examined more extensively by Rod Paton,[13] complemented by my own contextualisation.[14]

❖   ❖   ❖   ❖   ❖

## CONCLUDING THOUGHTS

IN READING THROUGH THE QUOTATIONS selected for this note, I was struck that only one included the word 'beauty', though much else could be said to infer it, taking 'beauty' to have a wider connotation than the visual.  Noticing the more painful stages of the journey to 'common ground', this line from Rilke may produce a spark:

> Beauty is the Terror we are only just able to bear.

---

13   Paton 2001
14   Ch.11

Finally, picking up the theme of modernity as representing the adolescence of Western humanity, addressed by Oliver Robinson in the same issue of Network Review,[15] I speculate that the mutual group regard and feelings of love discussed above may parallel in the individual the arrival of maturity with respect to loving oneself, thus then being able to love others without neediness, and to live in harmony with the world rather than fighting it.

---

Ten

## Spirit in Music

THE AIM OF THIS SHORT NOTE is, as a prelude to the extended
treatment in the following chapter, to explore ways in which we
experience or perceive spiritual affects in music—or indeed do
not, or had not recognized the full nature of our experiences.
Certainly I have played through, or composed to the end of,
particular pieces, and felt very satisfied without having any
conscious thoughts on spiritual aspects.

Maybe it's a matter of definitions: What do the words
'spirit' and 'spiritual' actually mean? They have many meanings, somewhat individual to us all. We could discuss this till
midnight and not get very far: deep philosophical explorations
always tend to lead us into much over-intellectualised considerations !

So simply—Spirit is what is not material: What about
mind? Ah, that also leads to the slippery slope of endless
discussion ! I have long had difficulty separating the concepts
of mind & spirit. So we will leave it here in that well known
phrase—Mind, Body, Spirit.

MUSIC. HOW DO WE RELATE THIS to the theme of spirituality?
Certainly music at the moment of its making is not material: I
refer to the conveyed sounds, not the propagating singers or

instrumentalists, and indeed nor the familiar recordings.

So is all music therefore spiritual?  This is where individual understandings come in.  Our personal thoughts and preferences define the answer, at least for ourselves.

As an example, ardent hard-rock aficionados apparently find the spiritual in succumbing to mind-blowing percussiveness.  For myself, though, any over loud music, particularly from over amplification (which tends to distort the natural flows of sound in the atmosphere without extraordinarily good sound technology) gives me nothing but a headache !  For such overtly 'in-your-face' sound production has no beauty for me, but is just noise, not music, designed to blow ones mind away !  But that is just *my* individual feeling on the matter.

What other perceptions are possible?  Very many, reflective of humanity's multiple developmental possibilities:  aspects of culture, personality and life experiences.

BEAUTY SEEMS TO NATURALLY ALIGN ITSELF TO SPIRIT.  This word, 'beauty', has been conspicuously missing from discussion of music since the collapse at the start of the 20thC of the four centuries old diatonic system of musical keys as the primary hostelry in town.

It is more than time to transcend the modernist fear of regression to attitudes culturally associated with supposedly defunct Romanticism.  Do we no longer have any cultural right to address the Romantic, in the proper sense of it as a comprehensively perceptive, and loving, approach to the reality of the world? This seems to be a parallel to the common attitude of banishing ideas of the spiritual side of things out of the modern, physically scientific materialist world. And yet we still love our partners, children, pets, gardens, nature at large ! Are not love and beauty aspects of the spiritual?

On a personal note, being independent by nature I have long wanted to create beauty using contemporary compositional techniques. Now that I have, I believe, reached some necessary plateau in my thirty year apprenticeship to the art and science of musical composition, the way is open for more beauteous work than I may have achieved before. Recent work for orchestral strings may hopefully validate that.[1]

WHEN WE SAY OF A PARTICULAR thing or idea, that it is *immaterial* to the concern in mind, we are, by the use of that word, relating to the all-too-common belief that physical, or material, reality is all there is: linguistic habits describe culture.

The profoundly gifted literary critic George Steiner, with his high intelligence and high intellectual integrity, found himself, in my reading of his book *Real Presences*, producing an argument about creative matters which was against his personal beliefs, and perhaps did not want, but he was none the less impelled on to the conclusion that of all the arts, music is the

1  See Score samples: *Touching the Deep*

closest to the divine.[2]  Because, he argues, it is intangible, and untranslatable.  And, before the invention of recording, evanescent.  This strikes a thoughtful note on our subject:  the spiritual as divinity—not specifically followed up here, but again we are viewing the languages we use, and meanings not thought out.

THERE ARE OF COURSE many gradations of what we may discern as spiritual in music, from 'practically nothing' to 'profoundly meaningful'.  I used that last phrase because just *there* is another definition of spiritual—that which gives depth and meaning, beyond intellectualism, beyond limited reliance on the verbal as truth statement.  'Profound' connotes depth.

Context provides clues towards listeners' expectations of overt or not so obviously discerned spirituality.  There might be an intention by, or a commission awarded to, a composer to write for a spiritual community, whether the liturgy of an established Christian Church, or Hindu chants from the Rig Veda, or setting poems or other texts of spiritual masters such as Rumi, or music at a pagan wheel-of-the-year ceremony—the assumption of 'wild music' in that context needs refuting, *so* commonly presumed:  I have been asked more than once for something meditational for such groups.

Here we have the composers' close association with a necessary feelingness needed in the true art of composition, working at paralleling the emotional/spiritual attitude the receivers of

2  Steiner, G. 1989

such music would expect.

AND MUSIC WITH NO OVERT CONNEXION to categories labelled spiritual may be, and should be anyway we might add, *inspired*, which literally means 'given breath': the breath of life. Depth psychology describes these non-materialities as access to the unconscious, the route to the (non-material image of the) 'bed-rock' of our being.

And that, in my opinion, is the route for all of us to search for and find connexion with the spirit, consciously or not.

I LEAVE IT THERE: Readers will amplify or disagree, according to where they have chosen to focus, where the act and art of living has taken them at this time, and where they are in relation to musical preferences and experiences.

And so to the amplification and contextualisation of these notes in Chapter 11.

# Eleven

# Musicmaking and Healing the Breach:[1]

## Mythmaking, Synaesthesia, and the Power of Sound

### PROLOGUE

THIS ESSAY, WRITTEN YEARS AGO, nevertheless seems to have even more cultural and therefore individual relevance now than it did in the writing of it.

We look at group musical improvisation from the points of view of the current demolition of our Western culture, viewed as a stage in mythmaking history, and from the modality of our personal and collective sensings in the sounding moments, ordinary and also non-ordinary, which at best create numinosity in the group and individual minds. Thus the improvisatory act can be seen as a beneficent factor working towards healing our Western world, which means ourselves within it, as we are integral to it.

The following poem was conceived back in the 1980s, a time when I was woken up to the terrible rent in the fabric of my own being, and beginning to perceive that that was (and is) not just my own tragedy, but endemic in our culture:

---

[1] First published in *Music & Psyche Journal*, Nov. 2001, pp27-39. slightly revised here.

I weary of lonely light years voyaging
To the far edge of imagination
In search of reality in truths
Which did not touch me.

In payment is the price
Of re-entry to the human race;
For all the loss of shared experience
And the ways of touching 'strangers' — all our kin.

Ask then shall we, from these unlooked for crossings
Of our orbits in this, life's galaxy
(Each high parabola overcharged)
 Careen away, decay?

Or, greatly fearing,
Suffer the sliding turning moment,
The terrible slingshot seizing us fast
Which hurls us to ourselves, and to each other?

❖   ❖   ❖   ❖   ❖

## MUSIC MAKING

THIS WRITING IS ABOUT ONE OF the modalities in which, in
small groups, concerted action springing from positive mutual
regard leads to collective experience of the numinous, communal touching of the divinity which is in us, and in which we

are. These are reflections on that form in which (O miraculous day!) I encountered the shared experience of the divine: group musical improvisation, as an un-egoic microcosm of life, and therefore a therapeutic environment for change.

Effort is required to achieve the depth of mutuality and trust wherein the numinous can appear, riding on the sounds and silences communally created: only sufficient time spent together, working to truly hear each other, can work this miracle. And the rightness of place, as well as time, also plays it's part.

Such music making has nothing to do with virtuosity: all of us in sufficient psychological health are innately musical, whether 'trained' or not. The purpose in such groups is to transcend or by-pass the ego in order to find the soul's purposes, a tender flower each one of us has in the recesses of our hearts. The yearnings there may be so sensitive that there are no words soft enough to express them. But deep longings can be expressed musically, wordlessly, within the holding crucible of a trusting group.

So if we can accept that we are our own myth-makers, that myth-making is the process by which we define ourselves and grow, then when we are truly and wholly gathered in the developed improvisation group we are myth-making via the collective engagement with sounding actions, which are simultaneously within the structure and part of it, the container and what is contained. We redefine ourselves, or we are 'soul making', in James Hillman's phrase,.

The myth involved here, I suggest, is precisely the view from each and every pair of eyes, the hearing in every pair of ears, and the feelings both given and received in every heart. And that sensing, feeling, is of ourselves as and in the group, in full flow of sound and balancing stillness of silence, perceived and contained in an aura of numinosity. We are not our ordinary selves. We have found connections between us which we have not experienced before. Not love in the common sense, but something crucially more impersonal, though as profoundly moving, as deeply felt, and unobstructed by the projections of ego.

Is this the true divine unconditional love?

When such work gels in this way we achieve what Mircea Eliade describes as an irruption of the sacred into the profane. That point of irruption is the hierophany.[2] We become that hierophany. We are, temporarily, a pantheon: we embody our own collective mythical event. This at its fullest expression is something so profoundly meaningful in the deepest, most embodied sense, that us ordinary mortals can bear it only briefly. We must, shortly, leave it: there is no appeal. But when we leave and return to 'ordinary' profane life, we nevertheless carry the memory of where we have been, what has

---

[2]  Eliade 1959

touched us in those small but infinitely large hours. This is our myth, our defining marker: we want to go there again: it points to where we wish whole-heartedly to be.

❖  ❖  ❖  ❖  ❖

## MYTHMAKING

IN THE EONS LONG LIFE OF THE WORLD SOUL, each great revolution on the axis mundi corresponds to an age in the slow working out of the destiny of our own ancient but still young species. And we find ourselves now at the edge of a new circum-vivification, mythos, noumenon, world view, opening up to our as yet uncertain gaze.

In this upcoming age we hope to find a healing of that great psychic rift, collective and individual, which has reached its greatest expression in the Western culture which now threatens to dominate (and decimate) itself, and the world. I refer primarily to the tremendous split in our culture which was given clear expression in the pact tacitly formed between the Church on the one hand, as self perceived guardians of learning during the long night of the middle ages, and Descartes on the other hand, as representative and successor to the Renaissance initiators of the revived personal urge towards intellectual, and secular, exploration.

The new scientific paradigm would be allowed to examine,

analyse, all matters material, leaving everything non-material in the hands of the religious authorities. From this separation there developed the denial by science of all that could not be measured, and from the dominance of that world view, the marginalization of the unseen world, the spiritual. This sundering of what is at root indivisible, wholly interconnected, appears as much in us, in our individual, our divided psyches, as it does in our collective culture.

It is a deep sickness at the heart of us all: now, though, becoming more commonly visible, as personal and also cultural wound. Since there is no sharp division between the ages, no clear cusp, developing strands of the new manifest like tender roots of the about-to-be world tree, young but strong, interlaced with the old crabbed woody anchors of the soon-to-be superseded. The last century has manifested, first isolated, then more and more examples of individual strivings towards that healing, in the arts and practices of inner care of Self and Soul, outer care for Mother Gaia.

It is all one: as above, so below, as the saying runs, means that each act or happening of connecting, re-joining, the formerly split within us has its parallel in the outer world. The workings of homeopathic remedies exactly illustrate this, pointing to the fact that every energetic function or dysfunction within us has its precise parallel somewhere else in the world, in other living beings or in apparently non-living materials.[3]

❖    ❖    ❖    ❖    ❖

MYTHOLOGICAL SEEKINGS

CAN WE EXPLORE FURTHER the meaning of that rift, which we feel to be connected to our deep sensitivities? Where does it come from? Can we find its essence in the world as it is? Or in the privacy of our psyches?

One route towards understanding is through mythology. There is a common usage of the term 'myth' which is pejorative. Myth is, in the mass media and in unconsidered speech, that which is unreal, perverse. I am refusing that definition, which I consider is an outcome of the split, the breach, we are considering. Myth here is the process by which "men everywhere have sought to relate themselves to the wonder of existence",[4] a vision of the divinity in which we live. This is as true for the youth deifying his football hero as it is for the acknowledged spiritual master, whose myths may be beyond our ordinary comprehension.

Joseph Campbell delineated the homogeneous mythology of the ancient, oriental and early occidental worlds, where

> Millenniums have rolled by with only minor variations played on themes derived from God-knows-when. Not so, however,

---

[3]   Whitmont 1993
[4]   Campbell 1976

> in our recent West where ... an accelerating disintegration has
> been undoing the formidable orthodox tradition, and with its
> fall, the released creative powers of a great company of
> towering individuals have broken forth: so that not one, or
> even two or three, but a galaxy of mythologies ... must be
> taken into account in any study of the spectacle of our own
> titanic age. (op cit)

In modern Western civilization the best of us pursue "the centering and unfolding of the individual in integrity". We self create our own individual variations on the themes of life's journey. The formerly dominant sphere of theology has been supplanted by "a totally new type of non-theological revelation" which has come from literature, secular philosophy and the arts, and has become "the actual spiritual guide and structuring force of the civilization." (op cit) Here are the sources of our myths: the poetic imagination as prophetic utterance; music as the art nearest to the divine; literature as descriptor of cultural possibilities and scrutinizer of the soul.

And so the great literary heritage of the Western world shines in our collective consciousness as illuminations of who we are, what we believe to be the essence of how our lives are lived at some more than mundane level. From Arthur's court and the Grail legend; through the unconscious chivalry of Don Quixote; the anguished stasis of Hamlet's self doubt; the Faustian legend of possible transcendence of avaricious self absorption through punitively costly and devilish bargains; the penetrating psychological perceptions embodied, particularly, in the works of the great nineteenth century Russian novelists; to the Joycean streams of consciousness and whatever coming after him will also capture the mythic imagination.

In music, great cathedrals of sound have been erected within the western polyphonic tradition representing the spirit of each passing age. Bach's soaring aspirations towards a transcendent Christianity; Handel's confrontation of newly becoming aware audiences with the power of his invention, the oratorio; Mozart the master of kaleidoscopic half shades of emotion, prefiguring the following century when man the all-possible was delineated by Promethean Beethoven. And on into the twentieth, the century of fragmentation, full of differential leadings, perhaps, as Rudolph Steiner delineated, the prelude to a new synthesis at the periphery of Europe. All represent aspects of the western psyche at the edge of the humanly possible. All the strands that make up the western collective soul are represented and reinforced by performances of the great musical works.

Another function of myth is prescription of a moral order:

> In Christian Europe, already in the twelfth century, beliefs no longer universally held were universally enforced. The result was a dissociation of professed from actual existence and that consequent spiritual disaster which, in the imagery of the

> Grail legend, is symbolized in the Waste Land theme. (op cit)

The common experience of many in the modern Western world, of growing up with an anguish of alienation from this world, attests to this split.

Leonard Shlain in a penetrating book[5] argues persuasively that the invention of writing in general, and the abstraction of that into the alphabet in particular, was instrumental in encouraging the development of unfelt left brain thinking. He points to this as a major factor in the rise of the masculine dominated culture we now feel (or hope) may be in process of supplantation or augmentation. Alphabetic writing is linear and abstract, requiring the left brain skills of precise visual focus and the analytical mode of thinking.

We had split ourselves in two, given honour to the new and powerful tool, and relegated to the darkness the shadow side of our culture and our psyches: all that was holistic, non-linear, intuitive. We projected that punitively onto those who to the masculinised mind most readily manifested those qualities: women.

So we have been living a lie, and also denying the source of our nourishment. Double jeopardy.

But in parallel these fractures enabled by their very presence possibilities of intellectual development, of knowledge

---

[5] Shlain 1998

which can be abstractly expressed as 'truth', embodied in the scientific world view. As is well known, this view has at its core a fundamental dissociation between observer and observed. Results of great value have come from this, but nevertheless the attitude exemplifies humanity in the great divorce of spirit and soul from materiality which we are here contemplating.[6]

And so arose the modern arts and therapies of psychology and psychiatry, needed crucially to help heal this breach in the fabric of our being.

And now we are into a new century and millennium, there is a growing perception of the value of sound, and so music, as energies wonderfully proficient in the task of bringing into connection and harmony that which has been torn asunder. When we talk, there is division: the speaker of the message, and they who receive it. Words define boundaries, separate. There is only a prescribed direction, from and to. When we collectively sing, or sound instruments, there is no 'message' in the verbal sense, there is 'only' the sound, produced by all, heard equally by all, tones transporting the verbal meaning into the innerness of what the word alone merely abstractly delineated. There is only one attitude, freely given: the duality of

---

[6] Of which there are signs now of some *rapprochement*, in the emerging findings of developed theoretical quantum physics relevant to physical body liminalities and the underlying bordering with non-physical energetics: See Knox 2023

from-and-to is transcended by the unity of the group in the sounding moment.[7]

❖  ❖  ❖  ❖  ❖

## PERSONAL MYTHS

IF MYTH DEFINES THE BOUNDARIES of what is truly human, a mirror which shows us where we are, and therefore where we may strive towards, then the nature of our own myths will be contingent on our own inner, linked psychological and spiritual growth—C.G. Jung's individuation.

Under the old Sumerian/Anatolian originated stasis, consequent supposedly on the invention of agriculture, where life was seemingly lived collectively under received certainties, the idea of individuation could not exist. People were *homo sapiens* indeed, but remaining harmoniously attuned to what we now, divisively, analytically, call 'nature', blindly separating off ourselves.

But in this Western world, where the idea of individuation has now its time as we move into the Aquarian Age, we perceive, and strive to come to terms with, the facts of differential growth among us. This means that my current mythology may be your clear vision, or the reverse. As we continue to grow, our perceptual boundaries widen. At those widened

_____

[7]  Zuckerkandl 1973

boundaries we may find fresh mysteries, requiring fresh mythmaking to provide something to grasp where clear thinking knowledge cannot yet apply, to recreate the Grail vision, the attractor towards the new goal for our spiritual journey. For feeling, from the heart, not analytical thought, is primary: we need imagery, not abstractions, to impel us on in our whole being.

That path of individuation, untrodden for each of us who set out along it, has its own excruciating rites of passage, expressed in legions of literary works: Shakespeare, Thomas Mann, James Joyce, and more recently William Golding and Robert Pirsig, to mention but a few. In music, Berlioz comes to mind, and Stravinsky, and in the visions of generations of authentic painters and poets striving to elevate personal angst into the universal, consciously or not.

❖   ❖   ❖   ❖   ❖

## SENSING

WHAT ACTUAL PERCEPTUAL POSSIBILITIES do we bring to coll-ective soul making, enabling conscious awareness of the experience? In group musical improvisations there is naturally hearing, but beyond that other senses play their part. Smell, and possibly taste, probably no more than in any other group situation, subliminally or even consciously inform us about the emotional states of our companions, part of our knowing the extent to which trust may be given in the situation. Vision and the tactile sense, however, have more direct roles, as has proprioception.

In the flow of active participation, as well as listening to what sounds others are making, we may also look at them, against the background of where we are working. Perhaps, mostly subliminally, we read facial expressions and body language, clues to the trajectories of supportive or interpolated sounds, data for our judgements on the placings of our own contributions, supporting the information from the sounds flowing all around.

The tactile sense, clearly, is an important part of the way we are able to play instruments. We feel our fingers on the keys, down the pipe, or on the strings and bow. This necessarily becomes unconscious as we advance our skills, so that precise and rapid physical movements are removed from the inefficiency of conscious control. It is though, I believe, also part of the way in which making music enhances our sense of well being, via the joyfulness of bodily movement: enhanced further when within the mutual support of the trusting group.

There are also internal sensations. The movements of muscles and joints as we bodily express the flows of sound, and the changes in breathing required by our alert state in general, and the needs of singing in particular, all are stimulants for our proprioceptors. In fact while making music we tend to breathe with the rhythms, whether or not we are singing or playing wind instruments. Our heart and pulse also do this, tending particularly to entrain with the beat, if there is one. Body sensations are integral to the wider experience. We may note here that one definition of the nature of spirituality is that we become more fully embodied, more fully focussed in the conscious, aware present moment, concerns with the regretted past and anxious future marginalized by the aliveness of now!

I note at this point merely that it is simply not possible to make music really effectively, whether improvised or precomposed, without being personally, in our innermost being, fully present.

But we are in essence creatures of vibratory energy. Atoms vibrate at enormous rates, causing the molecules they make up to vibrate coherently both mechanically and electromagnetically, but at a lower rate. Molecules emit, therefore, sound, and light in the ultra-violet range (UV), but both of very low intensity. Surrounding molecules entrain vibrations, imparting energy to the cells, and so to organs and through them to the body as a whole.

From atoms through to the whole body, vibrations occur in musically harmonic relationships, stepping down in frequency with increasing mass, as delineated by pioneer inventor Itzhak Bentov. This is where musical proportions originate.

The mechanical and electromagnetic vibrations find connections through the transducive qualities of a number of crystalline structures in the body, having similar properties to quartz, such as liquid crystals in the blood, salts in fatty tissues, colloidal structures of the brain, the pineal, and crystalline bone components.[8]

*Homo musicus* is a naturally resonating system, a system which reaches out beyond the body, via resonance with it's surrounding electromagnetic field (carrier of the aura?) to interact with the fields of other persons and things.[9] Not strictly a sense, and entirely unconscious except for certain sensitives who 'see' or otherwise sense auras, nevertheless it is another mode of connection between us, which will play its mysterious part in the group work whether 'seen' or not.

And in the developed group, in which all participants are fully focussed in the sounding moment, actively listening to each other, then in that heightened reality all senses may be consciously experienced more acutely, more finely discriminating, as the cleared pathways for the mythic connections discussed above. We may in that golden time once more become aware of our finger and tongue movements, without, however, regressing to the awkwardness of early learning: now it is no inhibition, it is an added richness. We may very

---

[8] Bentov 1978 – McClellan 1991

[9] Hunt 1996

well become aware of our heart beats and body movements as other modalities accompanying and enhancing the musical sounds. Hearing will become more acute, and at our fullest functioning, vision too. We achieve a multi-modal experience. We may perhaps, through heightened sensitivity, even become aware of the finer vibratory workings, maybe manifesting as intuitive knowledge of what someone else is about to do musically: we spontaneously, seemingly unexpectedly, connect our rhythms or pitches, for example.

On the other hand, if the circumstances are appropriate for a particular individual, the group music making can also overwhelm. The sounds themselves may transcend all other modalities, becoming an irresistible cathartic force.[10] The group may inadvertently sound the 'personal note' of an individual for whom some psychological, very probably traumatic block is approaching the moment of clearing. This may be not actually inadvertent, but a subliminal collusion, the group unknowingly preparing for the upcoming catharsis. I suspect this to be more likely if all in the group are vocalizing, most likely toning, though purposive drumming can also achieve the result. The topic is not enlarged further in this essay.

Heightened sensing will occur within what I have called the developed group, whether or not detailed recall is possible after the event. That depends on the energetic nature of the individ-

---

[10]   Neher 1962

ual heightened reality. This aspect is also not covered here. Valerie Hunt's pioneer creative work on the human vibrations of consciousness, investigations and intuitions much followed and amplified now, may be referred to for detailed information and comment.[11]

❖  ❖  ❖  ❖  ❖

## SYNAESTHESIA

BEYOND THE OBVIOUS senses and skills, what additional resources may there be to engage with the sounds we make?

Lyall Watson, multiply educated and trained explorer, describes and reflects on his sojourn in a small, remote, Indonesian fishing community. There he finds an extraordinary twelve year old girl, Tia, whose dancing with the village gamelan (an Indonesian metal orchestra) was astonishingly compelling.

Here he talks with her, walking on the beach. She is telling him the colours of sounds:

> "Brown is the sound of katak". Katak was the local toad [which] produced a derisory sound which was indeed rather brown.
>
> The idea was beginning to grow on me. 'What makes a black sound?'
>
> "Buffalo, and thunder." 'White?'

---

[11]  Hunt 1996

"The sea where it touches the sand."

Now I was really hooked. Tia was giving me these examples without hesitation, as though she were used to hearing sounds in colour. ... I thought of the tawny roar of a lion; of the scarlet scream of a macaw; of the deep bronze boom of an important bell, and of how the little ones that tinkled tended to be silver. 'All sounds have colours?'

"Astaga! You did not know?" 'No.'

"How can you listen to talk or music without colour?"

Her eyes were full of pity. "When the drums talk, they lay a carpet of brown, like soft sand on the ground. A dancer stands on this. Then the gongs call in green and yellow, building forests through which we weave and turn. And if we lose our way, there is always the white thread of the flute or the song to guide us home." [12]

He finds that all the other children also have this facility, though none so clearly as Tia. Reflecting on this, he comes to the conclusion that these are not mental associations, but complementary sensory inputs.

The study of synaesthesia attained its renaissance once Behaviourism was superseded together with the scientific refusal to recognize internal events. Findings following were that parallel sensing does exist, as distinct from imaginative figures of speech: an involuntary, unelaborated, and primarily emo-

---

[12] Watson, 1976

tional experience.[13]

Colour hearing seems commonest, others such as smell/ tactile sensations being less common. Even rarer are experiences involving more than two senses. There is no agreement among synaesthetes on the precise nature of their sensory parallels: for example the same sounds provoke different colours in different persons. The matter is quite idiosyncratic, and mysterious.

Seemingly female synaesthetes predominate, and the experience is prevalent in children before cultural learning obscures it, possibly 50%, adults maybe one third as many. As a group they may be more susceptible to 'unusual' happenings than the rest of us: clairvoyance, déjà vu, a feeling of 'presence'; maybe occurring more among more creative people. A number of artists, writers and musicians may have been synaesthetic, such as composers Liszt, Rimsky-Korsakov, Scriabin and Messiaen; poets Basho, Rimbaud and Baudelaire; painters Kandinsky and David Hockney; and novelist Nabokov, together with his wife and son—there would appear to be an inherited factor.[14]

A straw poll amongst people known to me revealed three female and one (slightly uncertain) male synaesthete. For one,

---

[13] As noted in fn 6, more recently quantum physics appears to be transcending the purely physicist's domain into affectual revelations in human consciousness, linked possibly to reports of increasing numbers of extraordinary children. As a literature example: Rodwell 2017 is carefully constructed and evidential. We are all inter-connected.

[14] Baron-Cohen & Harrison (eds) 1997

singer A.B., music evokes tactility *and* olfaction:

> When I hear music, I have strong tactile sensations though not
> necessarily in my hands. Music for me is characterised by
> being hard, soft, itchy, curved, stringy, sandpapery, etc. There
> is an olfactory link here too—Wagner's music definitely
> triggers an olfactory nerve. Some smells produce the same
> sensations in me as music, e.g. my hand-cream evokes the
> same sensations as certain kinds of abstract jazz, and roses the
> same sensations as Brahms symphonies (slow movements) ...
> The sensations are memorable, involuntary, the same each
> time I hear a particular piece of music. I've always had this
> kind of reaction, not realising that it was not absolutely
> 'normal' until I was in my 20s. Not imagined, not overwhelm-
> ing, and if I think about any feeling too hard, evanescent.

My own synaesthetic experience is completely singular (so
far). At a recital by the Garcia Conway Duo some years ago,[15]
in a small intimate venue, The Theatre, in the small town
Chipping Norton (Oxfordshire, UK), one of the works played
was Takemitsu's *Towards the Sea*, utilising the alto flute with its
warmly rich sound characteristics. Halfway through the piece
Takemitsu scored a handful of flute chords. Most wind players
tend to blow through chords, producing the effect of arpeggios,
but this player, Clive Conway, succeeded in the tricky task of
holding the breath steady in the exceedingly narrow pressure

---

[15] Gerald Garcia, *guitar* & Clive Conway, *flute*. I was reviewing for the local
paper.

band that produces a genuine chord. He succeeded for no more than a second for each rich chord of many sounds. As each one sounded, a colour spectrum appeared fleetingly in my head. Never before, not since !

What meanings can be drawn? Richard Cytowic suggests that synaesthesia may be a premature display to consciousness of an early stage in the sequence of normal cognitive processes which for most of us do not manifest until the sequence is concluded. He emphasises that the limbic system, associated with our emotions, has many more neural connections flowing *to* the neocortex, humanity's prideful centre of 'higher' cognition, than flowing *from*. This illustrates the reality of the statement made above that feeling is primary. During synaesthetic episodes blood flow to the *left* hemisphere cortex is (in at least one study) dramatically reduced, indicating some reduction in activity.[16]

Psychotropic drugs also induce the phenomenon. This is reported in many places, famously by Baudelaire on hashish. Also documented are synaesthetic components to shamanic experiences induced by plants, notably in Brazil where the vine Banisteriopsis is part of the 'brew'.[17]

So, while traditional peoples not overly dominated by Western culture may well retain experiences 'banished' by our

[16] Cytowic.' Synaesthesia: a review' - IN Baron-Cohen & Harrison 1997.
[17] Reichel-Dolmatoff 1997 & Roney-Dougal. n.d.

dangerously narrowed perspectives, as suggested by Watson's report, we in the occident may have largely lost it during cultural early social development and schooling, owing to overlaid inscribing of neural pathways relating to left-brained analytical thinking. *Homo logicus* is a dominant part of our cultural myths, as also discussed above.

Cytowic describes the process as the over-laying by more flexible, therefore dominating, cognition, and of course he is right as far as that goes. Lyall Watson surmised similarly a process of loss from childhood. And since left brain thinking is dominantly associated with the masculine, and therefore males, here may be an explanation why female synaesthetes predominate.[18]

Certainly the loss reduces the wealth of sensory experience, though an excess can interfere with cognitive functioning.[19] But could it be that we do not actually lose synaesthesia, so much as cease noticing, because it is not part of the prevailing definition of what humanly being is, not part of our culture and mythology. If this is so then it joins those other still small voices which it may take half a lifetime to take notice of, the voices of intuition, of 'that of God within', describe it how you will.

The route to uncovering, recovering, our forgotten perceptions will then be via finding our way below, or round, the

---

[18] McGilchrist 2009
[19] Luria. 'Synaesthesia' IN Baron-Cohen & Harrison 1997

rational brain to the other side of being, with which we know now our culture *must* reconnect, else our end may well be nigh. One arena for this is musical improvisation.

❧   ❧   ❧   ❧   ❧

## RECONNECTING WITH OURSELVES

IN THE WORK OF HEALING THE BREACH between estranged and impoverished mankind and the earth that in the rage of our estrangement we have raped and pillaged, is it too far fetched to suggest that as we reconnect with the true ground of our being, in parallel with that healing we may recover lost abilities and perceptions that maybe once we took for granted, or were simply unconscious of, which may, consciously perceived, marvellously enrich our interactions with the world?[20]

So, for those of us who work through the modality of sound at that breach, may we be conscious in all possible fullness of the vibrations of what we are doing, in hearing, vision and body awareness. But also that we who lack the conscious synaesthetic enrichment may become open to the possibilities of parallel sensings? Not in over confident materialistic minded either/or thinking, but with an attitude of 'allowing', maintaining and developing a certain watchfulness, an awareness at the edges of our consciousness in order to catch faint traces of

---

[20] A counterstroke to the threat of transhumanism.

the unexpected, gifts in embryo, and to hold these in memory, half understood, without attempted analysis, the better to relate to them when next they come. We may then become aware of what is in the spaces between our sounds and silences.

In that way we may help ourselves to open up to beneficial transformation, not caught unexpectedly by sonic *force majeure,* but when we are ready within our being, and only then losing ourselves in divinely elaborated energetic interactions with all we are really, truly connected to, in order to find ourselves where our souls reside—Into the labyrinth, with Orpheus as psychopomp !

The following poem with which we bring this essay to a close expresses reflections made regarding transformational experiences over several decades, which by the time of writing could be clearly seen for what they were: necessary, and inevitable, inner development:

> In that dark pool where coldest secrets are
> A needle point of heat has had to form:
> Through time unmeasured gains against the dark:
> Slow forms a roil, in long still waters born.
>
> Vague insubstantial presagers of change
> (Small messages let loose by turbulence)
> To consciousness by secret routes ascend,
> The fifty thousandth, only, making sense.

These signs, foreboding ends and startings, heed.
Do not think to quash that awe-ful pressure
(Formed sure, from in your life's beginnings, deep)
Which could then erupt in dreadful measure.

No, that fate upwelling fear not, nor blench.
Face fear and yield:  therein does lie your strength.


The last, appropriate word will be given to this Zen koan:

Take away sound and sense, and what do you hear?

# APPENDICES

# Appendix 1:  Jewitt Family

## ANCESTORS

I COME FROM A CREATIVE FAMILY:  grandfather Clement William
was a sculptor, his work rather limited by the 1st World War, a
fate suffered by many of his generation—too many up and
coming younger people coming from the war, proclaiming, and
needing, to be the new freshness; consequently grandfather
largely worked on war memorials.   Distant cousin Edward
Holmes Jewitt designed and created much of the stained glass
created in England in the first half of the 20thC.  Orlando Jewitt,
his brother Henry (my direct ancestor) and other family
members were wood engravers, Orlando and Henry living in
Headington[1] during Victoria's reign, overlapping the development of photography at that time.   They had moved there
consequent on much contractual work creating illustrations for
Oxford University Press books, and so are represented in the
John Johnson archives of that publisher.

The younger brother to Orlando and Henry, Llewellyn,[2]
lived in Derbyshire, leaving traces of his benefactive actions—
for example gifting drinkable water to the village of Winster by
pipe from three miles away (1871).[3]  His working life was *inter
alia* as a pioneering archaeologist, and his book on English
pottery, *The Ceramic Art of Great Britain,* was the standard work

---

1    Now a northern suburb of Oxford
2    No link with Welshness identified:  there were though several other
     brothers, and inventive naming.
3    Winster was a mining village:  the local water contaminated by lead ore etc.

for more than 30 years at the end of the 19th century. He wrote several other books, including *Grave Mounds and their Contents; Half Hours with English Antiquities; The Stately Homes of England, 2 vols* (many of those reported there no longer exist); *Derbyshire Ballads; and Black's Guide to Derbyshire*, a fascinating historic guidebook, armed with which I observed subsequent development in that county: little change above the ground floor—new shop fronts there in towns and villages.

Further back in this lineage is the collectable ceramic *Jewitt Plate* made in 18thC Sheffield. Apparently there were no musicians reported in previous generations—that trait seemingly came through my mother's family, if genetics is the only route, which I doubt: two modest working violinists are known of in the Charles family, three or four generations back from the 21st century—when a child, my mother was nicknamed 'Charlie'.

## CLEMENT'S RESUMÉ

Bmus obtained in 1997. PhD awarded in 2006 (aged 65) while teaching at Birmingham Conservatoire. Founder member of *Music & Psyche* in the late '90s: ran improvisation workshops under that banner in various places in the UK and Republic of Ireland until 2008, some with colleagues, some without. Ceased formal employed work then owing to illness. Associate Editor of the *Music & Psyche Journal*, which lasted for 4 issues—there were simply not sufficient writings found, despite Calum Mac-

Donald, the then editor of the journal *Tempo,* remarking that we filled a needed niche. Several contributions from me appeared in *Tempo,* including *Music at the Bauhaus.*[4]

Until cessation of composing I was an active member of the Severnside Composers Alliance, based in Bristol: I had come south-west to live with my third wife, Margaret in Gloucestershire. Recent professional performances: *Canto* for violin and piano with Madeleine Mitchell and Geoffrey Poole—3 performances, 2016 & 2017. And some small works at Severnside DIY concerts in 2018 and 2019 featuring the singer Marianne Lihannah and pianist and clarinet player Matthew Heyse-Moore. Stasis 2020 into 2022 . . . And beyond, as seems likely at the time of writing. Maybe.

---

4    This will be included in the 2nd small book on matters musical.

# Appendix 2: 70th Birthday Celebration Concert

**I**T ALL WENT SPLENDIDLY WELL: Held in the *Jaqueline Du Pre* music room in Oxford, during a rather stormy evening, the Astaria String Quartet and the Pavlova Wind Quintet provided masterly musicianship, craftsmanship and sheer dedication: I couldn't have expected more. And Wendy Nieper: well, those who haven't heard her before are always astonished by her superbly felt singing, wide range and evenness across that range. And contrary to that old joky prejudice, she is not 'just a singer', but a very discerning musician ![1] She is such a very busy professional singer, I feel quite warmly affirmed by how readily she agreed to sing for me.

Raymond Head, composer, conductor, teacher, an all round experienced musician and long a colleague and friend, wrote:

> What a special night it was! I thought your pieces came over really well especially the wind quintet and string quartet. You were lucky with the performers too. They were a very committed bunch of musicians and had obviously worked hard on your pieces. I have to say that I think the string quartet was as near being a masterpiece as it is likely to get.

Wendy commented on that: "I think I might agree that the 2nd half string quartet is close to a masterpiece. It was truly wonderful."

The first half string quartet was an early tryout for that instrumentation, consisting of a single movement in 3 sections,

---

1  See Ch 3 p.34/5 for her comment on contemporary song writing.

duration 8 minutes, titled *Be Calm, Move Gently*. In the second half was the later quartet No.2, in four somewhat traditional movements, reflecting in its thematics a harking back somewhat to earlier diatonic quartet writings. So I titled it *That Which Was*. See the *Score Samples* section.

On Wendy, Raymond wrote:

> I thought Wendy's singing was great and I kept wondering why she sounded so different from the last time I heard her, so rich and deep in the lower register—and then you said she had married. Therein lies the answer !!! The Two Songs from *The Night Sea* sounded better last night than before and *And Not Another Man* had some gorgeous harmonies in it.

She had married one month prior to the concert, and at its close we presented her with a card and a huge bunch of flowers in commemoration of that. The usually unfazed by anything Wendy looked delightfully embarrassed !

Sean Gilde, the cellist, wrote on behalf of the Astarias:

> It was a real challenge for us to get to grips with your music, but one that ultimately was very satisfying as there were so many wonderful textures and moods in all of the works. Thank you for choosing to have us play and premier your compositions especially as you also introduced us to such a brilliant vocalist!

Christopher Britton, flute, wrote:

> I thought it was a really lovely occasion—so much warmth in evidence. I thought the choice of venue very appropriate. The Jacqueline du Pre has the advantage of considerable intimacy.

Old friends Mike and Anne Bardsley ran the affair on the day, so I could relax in order to actually HEAR the music, instead of constantly worrying about details. I found myself several times astonished—how did I write that? I guess I had been hearing with my inner ear, while not entirely conscious of that, simultaneously applying the conscious compositional techniques.

Several people contacted me beforehand to cry off owing to "coughing for England", in the words of one, and so did not come. What good friends I have. There was not a single cough or sneeze throughout the concert. The audience was not large, but very attentive, mostly old and new friends: very few were not already known to me,. And two of my children came. Very heartening to receive their support.

Musicians in the audience: apart from Raymond Head, mentioned above, there was Gilbert Biberian, formerly guitar professor at Trinity College, London who said "where did you get such splendid players?" He made a point of catching Wendy. I thought there was something in the wind there, which later manifested in her working with him.[2] And Bill Brookman, a multi instrumental musician (with clown skills too) who took street theatre events into troubled regions of the world, like Haiti, using creativity as a balm. He said, solemnly, lugubriously, "We are very, very impressed: we will come to the 100th!" About a third of the audience consisted of musicians, all very happy with the concert !

2  Sadly, he died after a fall in February 2023.

## Post Scriptum

There should have been an 80th birthday concert. That birthday was in December 2020. The plan was therefore abandoned owing to the pandemic lockdowns. Further comment is not necessary.

# Appendix 3. Three composers muse on life and Western art music:

## Mechanisms and Shadows

IN AUGUST 2002 AN ARTICLE BY Geoffrey Hindley was posted to the Music-Psyche Yahoo Discussion Group entitled *Keyboards, Cranks and Communication: the Musical Mindset of Western Technology,* which proposed that *'the mindset of western art music is at the core of modern world techno-culture.'*[1]

The argument was supported by examination of the singularity of western art music, which is distinct from all other 'high musical traditions' in being polyphonic, using 'unnatural' tuning, a fixed semitone sequence, pre-composed closed forms, an elaborate and highly prescriptive notation, and a machine as its chief instrument.

The history of western mechanistic instruments begins with the hydraulis, which metamorphosed into the organ, that *'uniquely western machine … [which was for centuries] the largest mechanism, even including the city or cathedral clock, in any European town.'* Next came the organistrum and its popular successor the hurdy-gurdy, offering evidence for the development of the crank in Europe, and then the accordion, taken up by the European folk music tradition which has for centuries welcomed mechanistic music making—the only one in the

---

[1]   From ICON—Journal of the International Committee for the History of Technology, Vol.3, 1997. Here and following, the quotes from Hindley's article are in italics.

world to do so.  And then of course to clavichords, harpsichords and pianos, the keyboard applied to strings.

Among other contrasts, Hindley also adduces to support his thesis the immediacy of sound to the senses as compared to vision, natural tunings versus tempered, and the maintenance of tradition as prime operative in all musics except for the western, which privileges innovation.  The latter is supported by complex highly specific notation which, in the context of European technological strivings may be seen also as a manifestation of that Western holy grail, the labour saving device, enabling performers to escape the chore of learning the music, thus releasing energy for novelty.

The article fanned sparks in the psyche of the Canadian composer John Burke, and the resultant 'channellings' (his word) in turn drew responses from Maxwell Steer and Clement Jewitt.  The three of us found we were sailing in formation across the same ocean signaling energetically to each other (via e-mail).  These interchanges we now present to you, slightly edited, feeling that the triangular pyramid with Hindley at the apex was an alchemical furnace which 'had us in the grip of our collective daemon' (John's words again) crystalizing nuggets which here we share.

### Where from and wherefore? Thoughts on Hindley

*I shall argue that the mechanical habit of mind; that the characteristically western pattern of thinking in terms of progressive dev-*

*elopment; that the habit of innovation; that even the basic principles of*
*'R & D', originated with the new mindset evolved in and by the*
*western European tradition of art music. If the proposition be accep-*
*ted, it will be seen to be no coincidence that music and technology are*
*the two all pervasive western exports to the world at large.*

**JB (John Burke):**[2] And it therefore stands to reason that
Germany, which has produced some of the greatest machinery
in the world, should have produced some of the greatest music.
It has also produced in recent times some of the worst abuse of
patriarchal power in the world—the shadow side of the mus-
ical/technological marvel. One wonders whether there must be
some mysterious linkage in these three elements.

**MS (Maxwell Steer):** My own insight into this strange con-
catenation was guided by an art exhibition that visited
Birmingham a couple of years ago called The Kingdom of the
Soul. It featured the German tradition of metaphysical or
symbolist art that stemmed from Arnold Böcklin. The catalog
explained that he was the focus of a 19th century group of ex-
patriates who thought of themselves as the DeutschRömer, that
is, the spiritual-cultural heirs of the mythical Holy Roman
Empire that originated with Charlemagne.[3]

Its fascinating to listen (*inter alia*) to Schoenberg's *Gurre-
lieder* & nearly all Mahler and hear being 'yearned into life' that
very quality of nostalgic fantasy about a mythic courtly past

---

[2]    Died in middle years 2020
[3]    So pregnantly illustrated in the original paper: *A court eulogist boasted that*
*now even the organ 'the only reason why the people of Constantinople felt*
*themselves your master [O Caesar!], is represented in Aachen'.*

that the Nazis were to load with such deadly freight a couple of decades later as the 'third' empire. Nor should it be forgotten that in Shaw's paean to all things Nietzschean, *The Perfect Wagnerite*, of which he published five versions 1898-1923, he is extraordinarily explicit in anticipating the arrival of a 'super-man consciousness' within persons (as enlightened as GB Shaw) who could be relied upon to act 'rationally', having dispensed with the mental fog of religion and social convention! How much did it surprise Shaw, I wonder, that it was Nazism rather than the Bloomsbury group which proved the more pregnant force?

**CJ (Clement Jewitt):** Another vector to this could be that, if the national temperament of Germany may be allowably, if sweepingly, categorized as predominantly based on the intellect, with *feeling* relatively undifferentiated, as contrasted with the French national temperament predominantly centered on the feelings—the finely differentiated feeling tones in classic Moulin Rouge presentations as compared to the mug-waving popular songs at the lads' night out in a Bavarian Bierkeller—which is by no means to critique the power of the Gallic intellect, only its character—then we have a possible route to comprehension, given the I hope widely accepted understanding that thinking ungoverned by feeling is unprotected against anti-humanitarian tendencies, leading at worst to outright evil in the name of some 'principle', but leaving the positive creative side of intellect still free, not necessarily in the same individual.

Perhaps supporting this, Leonard Schlain in *The Alphabet*

*versus the Goddess*[4] presents a comprehensive and quite per-suasive argument for the notion that the onset of specifically alphabetic writing, totally abstract once the Greeks had stripped the remaining pictographic vestiges from it, and situated at the very centre of the culture, provoked predominance of left brain analytic thinking, required to comprehend the writing. And hence by an argument I think it not necessary to elaborate here, lead to, or reinforced, dominant patriarchy.


## European Zeitgeist

IN THE GREAT MONODIC TRADITIONS *the art of the musician consists in exploration and exposition of the sound world that lives in the mystic body of wood, gourd or shell strung with gut. Compared with the keyboard and the festooned mechanisms of western wind instruments, these were organic members of the natural world. Modifications of their structure were, if not blasphemous, then pointless since the vocation of the musician was to enter and understand their musical world and not to 'improve' it.*

**JB:** If a culture is producing the best high performance motor cars in the world, it is literally trying to go someplace. If it is similarly producing the best high performance music in the world, then it would seem evident that *it is* trying to go someplace. But where? What has motivated this extraordinary phenomenon of musical progressive development, innovation, inexorable expansion of ways and means, with its attendant

---

[4]    Schlain 1998

wrenching changes of psychic state—not to mention the exponential inflation of the ego of the art music composer—that is unique to the West? Where did we think we were going? What did art music think it could do?

**MS:** It thought it could be God! Certainly, in their own way both Wagner and Berlioz thought that, Beethoven having finally burst the shackles of regal and religious patronage, they were free to create music that truly expressed the scope of man as the supreme being of the universe. How interesting tho, that both were deeply 'infected' by their own gods, that is, that the personal psychology of both men was deeply interpenetrated by a level of perennial consciousness—the dear old Collective Unconscious—that gave them a sense of 'the sublime', as the Gothick movement called it.

*In such traditions, through the bard, humankind could approach the music of the spheres, the musical structure of the world. The acoustic mysteries of interval and mathematics were linked to the secrets of the universe. The almost innumerable gradations of vibrational pitches between the unison and the octave were ordered into complex scales – Arab maqqam, Indian raga and Greek tropoi ('tropes') or 'modes' as they are called – each held to embody and express its own microcosm of sentiment, mysticism or expression.*

**JB:** What was the metaphysical aspiration of Leonin and Perotin when in the 12th century they began 'turbocharging' the plainchant with their duplum, triplum and quadruplum organum? Were they intuitively aware of the energetic healing properties of chant[5] and were trying to 'amp up' the effects for the benefit of their parishioners? Was art music in the West now assuming the daunting task of spiritual transformation that in the East was addressed through yoga and meditation? In the spiritual technologies of Tibet the peaceful and wrathful deities are processed internally; in the West such things might be mythically worked out in chromatic harmonic splendor on the opera stage at Bayreuth. Or were we (to return to the engineering metaphor) blindly supplanting the former primal esotericism of the heart with a 'guy thing' esotericism of the head?

Has not the overly yang trajectory of art and science in the West—with all its patriarchal excess—just about run its course? Is it not time for a massive re-infusion of the healing yin energy that with those first contrapuntal experiments 800 years ago at Notre Dame has increasingly retreated underground, to become the disenfranchised, unlived life of Western music, resurfacing in shadow form in Mozart's *Queen of the Night* and the lunar feminine eruptions of Schoenberg's *Pierrot* and *Erwartung*?

If we approach the entire history of Western classical music in Jungian terms, as one would view the life cycle of an individual, one could perhaps see plainchant as the stage of infancy or unconscious wholeness, unconscious egolessness. Music's subsequent technical expansion could then be seen as the process of individuation, the development of conscious ego,

---

[5]  As revealed in the famous incident when Dr. Alfred Tomatis restored the depleted health of the Benedictine monks by returning them to their regimen of daily chanting

adamantly establishing one's place in the world. At some point this external power, outward bound agenda inevitably runs into trouble (or as Joseph Campbell put it: having reached the top of the ladder one realizes it's against the wrong wall), which seems to happen around the time of Wagner's *Parsifal*. The subsequent midlife crisis of 20th century music is the story of a confused and ofttimes desperate attempt to locate, reclaim and integrate a newly empowered feminine energy into a newly defined transformative role for serious music—a task as yet incomplete, but as we enter a new millennium perhaps within our grasp.

At that point we will have come full circle—the fruition of the Hero's Journey—returning now to a new place of conscious egolessness, our previous efforts toward external power having been transformed into a healing quest for authentic power, power for the benefit of others. And with it the best response to the question of why Western music, unlike its Eastern counterpart, left the safety and security of the contemplative tradition of plainchant to take a millennium-long walk on the wild side.

**CJ:** Music history as Jungian life cycle! Indeed! As a devout Jungian myself (apologies Carl, I know you refused the appellation) I have been in the last several years working with a Jungian based model of the psyche,[6]

Schlain's thesis could be applied to the adventure of Leonin

---

6    Applying it to composers' procedures, the dynamics of musical
     performance and audition, and to the forms of written music. See Hill 1992,
     and Music Book.2.

and Perotin as an aspect of the reasons why, having in mind Hindley's gloss on the 'verticalizing' of the musical concept from its purely horizontal, linear shape. The masculine, left brain emphasis required for written text comprehension now applied to music, by intellectual experimentation.

**MS:** I'd hazard they were partly having fun with new (conceptual) toys but also that they felt they were contributing to the advancement of Christendom. It was the high period of 'scholasticism' in Paris—of which they were the musical counterpart. Its also the period from which the earliest European (religious) dramas date. In the post-millennial period there seems to have been a genuine Europe-wide religious fervour (or outpouring of spirit, depending on how you look at it), of which Hildegard is a preeminent example, which expressed itself materially in cathedral building and, alas, the Crusades. In a way the music could be looked at as reflecting the imperialism of the age, just as the bombastic power of the symphony orchestra did the aspirations of the 19$^{th}$ century.

**CJ:** And which may be also associated with the masculinisation (hence imperialism) resulting from the re-literacising of Europe then gathering way, at least among the educated cultural leaders, following the so-called Dark Ages when only largely closeted monks kept the literary tradition barely alive, but the rest of the people (happily?) lead lives without reading matter. We may note the at least equal status of women then, recorded in the Troubadour tradition as well as historical facts about noted women occupying powerful positions. This too is part of Schlain's argument.  So the 'guy thing' would naturally follow from that reassumption of literacy, appropriated by the masculine.

## Midlife crisis

MS: WOULDN'T YOU SAY THAT a 're-infusion of the healing yin' is already in process?  Its interesting that D'Indy bought early instruments and made students of the Schola Cantorum play on them.  Perhaps that's what attracted Satie to it?   Also that Respighi, whose sound-world is synonymous with opulence, collected early instruments and loved to play chamber music on them.   Then again there is the extraordinary conjunction of Dolmetsch developing the instruments needed for a kind of musical pre-Raphaelitism in Haslemere against the backdrop of Europe's collective self-destruction in WW1.

I would locate the first explicit inciting act of this 'phase-reversal' to Debussy's encounter with the Javanese Gamelan at the Paris Exposition of 1898(?)—so you could say that while the phallocratic dynamic of European 'civilisation' foreshadowed by masculine scientific objectivism in the $11/12^{th}$ centuries reached a peak, musically, with the Nazi Strauss, a counterbalancing movement had already arisen with Debussy's insistence on the primacy of feeling, and his assertion of the significance of subjectivity.

I would make the case that this 'new' strand in Eurocentric music, which arose spontaneously in several unrelated composers (Debussy, Ives & Varèse, not to mention Stravinsky) was a restatement of the irrational first brought into European consciousness by the Gothick movement in the late 18$^{th}$ century, where Walpole & Beckford, acting independently, apparently found that the searing rationality of Enlightenment science left no room for imagination or personal expression. Searching for what they called 'the Sublime', that is, a validating sense of otherness within, they re-articulated the age-old human need for non-rationality as the womb of creativity—as Lorca said, 'duende [twilight, ambiguity] alone makes us live.'

**CJ:** A clear case of the universal duality principle that everything contains, or provokes, its opposite. And my thoughts above on national character apply to your remarks on Debussy (who was taken to hear the Gamelan by that literary comedian Satie). Can we trace something of the long heard differences between German and French music (dismissive German historians, etc) with this in mind? In other words Debussy as the continuator of tradition as well as the innovator.

Which leads to Part 2 of these musings, to be published in Musings on Music Bk 2. Three Composers Muse is then primarily concerned with aspects of contemporary Western new music culture: Ours and others' views.

# Encomiums and Reviews

From *Dr Rod Paton*, University of Chichester, England

CLEMENT JEWITT'S COMPOSITIONS demonstrate a fertile imagination, a high level of musical understanding and an exacting attention to details of technique. The genre in which he creates is modernist but entirely accessible and whilst his works demonstrate commitment to a personal path they also stem from a deep sense of engagement with performer and potential audience.

Furthermore, his music is also engaged with a "new paradigm" of aesthetics which places creative process at the heart of psychic development, both individual and collective. He combines an analytical understanding of musical process with a dedication to philosophical, psychological and humanitarian issues, and demonstrates considerable skill in both areas.

From *Dr Sydney Baggs*, New South Wales, Australia

YOUR MUSIC IS EVOCATIVE AND HAUNTING. It has a mysterious quality that is very appealing. [Personal communication after listening to two CDs of my music. Dr Baggs is the author of *Underground Housing for the Australian Arid Region*, and with Joan Baggs *The Healthy House*, and *The Underworld in Myth, Magic and Mystery*, and other books.]

From *Diana Burrell*, Guildhall School of Music and Drama.

CLEMENT IS A FINE MUSICIAN with far-reaching interests and a wide experience of all kinds of music-making. Each new work shows an ever-increasing sophistication in scope, form, instrumental colouring, etc.

## On *The Night Sea: Aspects of an ordinary life*

THIS IS A RICH, colourful work, brimfull of life and energy! A project which has occupied its composer's thoughts to a greater or lesser degree for the last 20 years or so, it goes right to the heart of creation, celebrating humankind's place in the cosmos and illuminating the masculine and feminine within each of us. Out of the many scores I've looked at over the last couple of years, here is one I'd really like to hear, for in an age addicted to irony and superficiality, this is a strong, generous piece of music which truly deserves a performance. I so hope this is achieved.

*Diana Burrell*

[See Ch.3 for comments on this piece by Jonathan Harvey & others.]

## On *Invocations to Archangels*, 2002.

THE MUSIC IS EVOCATIVE AND HAUNTING. The sounds recalled me to a symphony of souls I heard while in an altered state—the sounds of innumerable souls expressing the inexpressible—yearning, awe and mystery, & the separation that seeks union.

*Shulamit Elson*[1]

I CHANCED (!) TO SWITCH ON the radio this morning and at once

---

1 The author of *Kabbalah of Prayer: sacred sounds and the soul's journey*.

found myself listening utterly spellbound to something profoundly beautiful, this hauntingly beautiful mysterious sound
with the moving text as a powerful 'undercurrent'.

Acquaintance *Sue Thoma*

HAS A UNIQUE FLUIDITY and three-dimensional transcendental
quality to its use of voices.From *Katherine Howard*, painter

On ***But we must still be seeking?*** Wind quintet.

THE 2001 BIRMINGHAM CHAMBER MUSIC PRIZE went to the composer Clement Jewitt, formerly of Oxfordshire, but now a resid-
ent of Birmingham.

One might be forgiven for thinking that a new wind quintet
in a programme that also included works for the medium by
Hindemith, Ligeti, Nielsen and Janácek would be lost, but it
says a lot for Jewitt's piece that this was not the case. Working
in a post-serial idiom, without a trace of Post-Modernism, he
has written an undeniably effective work. How refreshing not
to have another chirpy British quintet, full of jaunty tunes and
perky rhythms of the kind that once we were so plagued by!

In a programme note, the composer has suggested that in
his piece various forms of community are put forward and musically discussed: sometimes there are arguments, sometimes
players move away from the group to ponder their musical fate,
as it were. At other times they move around in two or threes,
always pushing the scalic modes and rhythms to further extremes. So from simple beginnings the language is modified

and expanded, often very lyrically but also contrapuntally, to take account of the new dialectics that are being formed. In the end 'they sing the same song, calmly, each with his/her own individual voice contributing to the whole'. *Raymond Head, Tempo*

On **Chechnya Story, 1997** *(text by Olivia Ward, Toronto Star)*

MOST STRIKING MELODRAMA, but any association of Jewitt's sensitive expressions with that over-used term with its meaning today is wildly inappropriate. Maybe [the] clearly sincere text (not originally intended for musical setting) doesn't quite match the intensity of the beautifully unfolding music, but together with it combines to an overwhelming statement of compassion. Words set by composers like Schubert and Bach become transfigured by the process of being adorned with music, and for one of those rare times in my life, I felt that such comparisons are anything but ridiculous.

*Stephen Daw, Coventry Evening Telegraph.*

THE DARK VEIL OF DESPAIR that is Chechnya[2] was pulled back for all to see last night in a musical performance: ... A bittersweet symphony to the final note ... left a Canada House audience haunted by its tragic tale of freedom fighters who find love in the overwhelming presence of death. Jewitt's brooding score formed a harrowing backdrop to the spoken word delivery of Ward's text by British Actors Corinne Lang and Dawn Foxall.

*Mitch Potter, Toronto Star.*

---

2    NOTE: This was after the country had been destroyed by the Russians, and before the extremist Moslems moved in with supposed 'rescue' money.

I LOOK BACK TO THE Chechnya piece as one of the most interesting and stimulating pieces in which I was privileged to be involved and thank you sincerely for that memory.

*Corinne Lang*, pers com.

On *Knit Up the Ravell'd Sleeve of Care*. 11 bassoons,
1 contrabassoon.

STEVEN LLOYD GONZALEZ DIRECTED TWELVE student bassoonists in the premiere of Clement Jewitt's *Knit up the ravell'd sleeve of care*, substantial and darkly atmospheric as various combinations emerge physically and musically from the pools of the unconscious mind.     *Christopher Morley, Birmingham Post*

On the CD *The Coming of Light*

THE MUSIC ON YOUR NEW CD is absolutely wonderful; heart soaring, expansive and delicate at the same time—exquisite. Heartfelt thanks and ongoing murmurs of appreciation.

*Deirdre Burton, playwright, song writer & wisewoman*

# Score samples

## Invocations to Archangels:

composer's text: choral version: 1st & last pages

duration c. 8'

# The Night Sea: Aspects of an ordinary life
## First section 1st + last pages & last section 1st + last page

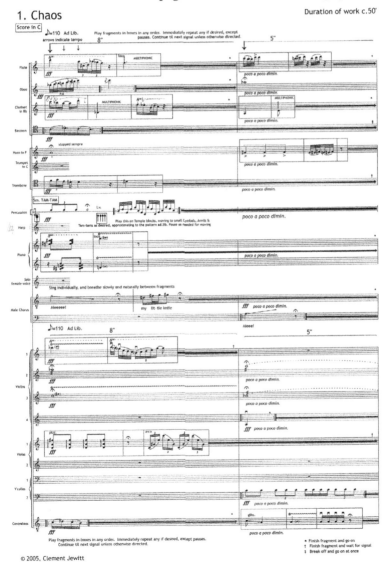

© 2005, Clement Jewitt

And then after eight poems, each one embedded in appropriate instrumental settings, plus four instrumental interludes, the last section and poem arrives, approaching 50 minutes later. This is a setting of *i thank You God for most this amazing day,* an e.e. cummings poem.

The first and the last pages of §15 are exampled below

## 15. The End is the Beginning

Sparkbrook, Kenya & Uganda,
Dec. 2003 — April 2005,
with some additions & changes,
Aug. & Nov. 2008. CJ

# Touching the Deep - orchestral strings

## That Which Was - String Quartet

# SONGS
## James S. Kavanaugh - But a Part of It All

duration c. 9'

## 1. Sadness is But a Part of it All

Sad-ness  is  but  a  part  of  it  all  part - of  it

all  Com-ing —  so  re - lent - lessly

re - lent-less- ly  in the  morn-ing —

'Sadness is but a part of it all' and 'Time to start anew' from 'Quiet waters' by permission
of the publishers: Stephen J Nash Publishing, PO box 7606, York PA 17404, USA

Marion Griffin - And Not Another Man (String Quartet No.1)

2. He would send me

# Richard Eberhart - Rumination (with SQ)

duration 15'

When I can hold a stone within my hand
And feel time make it sand and soil, and see
The roots of living things grow in this land,
Pushing between my fingers flower and tree,
Then I shall be as wise as death,
For death has done this and he will
Do this to me, and blow his breath
To fire my clay, when I am still.

From Collected Poems 1930-1960. Oxford U.P.-USA.
"The permission is granted for use of the poems in the presentation of your cycle
entitled Aspects of the Night Sea Crossing." Richard B. Eberhart.

## Milton Godfrey - Come With Me

## Ruth Pitter - If You Came

If you came to my___ se-cret glade, Wear - ry - with

heat, I would set you down in the

shade I would wash your feet

I would wash___ your feet

## Mark Strand - The Coming of Light (with SQ)

# Recordings references

NOT ALL MY COMPOSITIONS have been performed, and not all those that have were recorded. Additionally, a few recorded pieces are under restrictions in the matter of usage—the performers who played in the recorded concert had refused to allow any *ad hoc* usage, perhaps not feeling that their renditions in the concert were good enough, which is very fine, and quite possibly they were expecting some tightly controlled studio recordings in the future. These matters were unspoken, but were deducible.

Nevertheless, the recordings noted below are deposited in the website which was created to house them. To access the recordings, cite
https://clementjewitt.co.uk/recordings-1/ for the quartet recordings, and
https://clementjewitt.co.uk/recordings-2/ for the songs. Click on the head text to move from one page to another.

The titles of each recording can then be seen on the web page.

The performers on that CD were, firstly, the very versatile singer Wendy Nieper, who as a classical singer has appeared with well known European and American orchestras. She has premiered many contemporary songs, including several of Clement Jewitt's. As a jazz singer she has  sung with many of the country's leading jazz musicians including Digby Fairweather, Denys Baptiste, and Dame Cleo Laine.

And the Astaria String Quartet: *violins* Shulah Oliver & Kelly McCusker; *viola* Kate Bickerdike; *cello* Sean Gilde. Inspirational and innovative, the Astaria String Quartet continues to explore less well known works for string quartet, and also aspects of audience participation with their 'Evening of Requests' and the commissioning of new music by local composers. They were awarded an 'Arts 4 All' Grant from the National Lottery to study with the distinguished chamber musician Gábor Takács-Nagy. Their first album, *Fiesta*, celebrated Spanish and Latin American music and included the first recording of Piazzolla's *'Tango Ballet'*.

At the time of the recordings they were Quartet in Residence at Huntingdon Hall Worcester, England.

www.astariastringquartet.com

And here they are at the recording of *The Coming of Light*—with myself and Wendy Nieper:

THE PIECES ARE, IN ORDER, ON clementjewitt/recordings-1/

**String Quartet No.1** (this is as cited on the web page, which will be so for all here following) consisting of 3 movements, each of which has a sung text: three poems by Marion Griffin, under the title:

### And Not Another Man:

**1st movement.** *All My Suffering* **- 5.06'**

All my suffering finds its
          meaning
In the fewness of the words
You need to tell me
Yours . . . once only.
All the lovers I took and
          abandoned
All the discarding
I underwent meant only
That I did not have to have
You . . . again.

Sometimes choosing has been
          painful
Losing out
But gaining ground
So that I could stand firm
And not choose
You . . . always.
I may not persevere now
I am safe to wish again
So knock on my door
Smile me your grin
And I will go with
You . . . for a while.

**2nd movement.** *He Would Send Me* **- 2.01'**

He would send me running
Up grassy banks ahead of him.
If I had taken a tumble
He would have been there
To break my fall
To kiss my grazes.
And so I ran
Made the top
Laughed and panted
While he
Took the last stride to join me
And take my hand again.

**3rd movement.** *And Not Another Man* **- 4.35'**

Be beautiful, and be the one you are
Be kind, and be a friend when friends are found
Be brave, and you will travel near and far
Be careful as you're testing out the ground.
Be boyish and delight girls with your charm
Be manly and you'll feel a woman's power
Be courteous when you take a lady's arm
Be elegant when handing her a flower.
Be spirited and dare to go too far
Be circumspect when thinking what to say
Be honest when the wounding leaves a scar
Be patient when the moment comes to pay.
Be ever wonderful, believe you can
Be your sweet self and not another man.

NEXT IS **String Quartet no.2**, titled: *That Which Was.*

This work has a long history, originating in some sketches done in the late 1980s which did not quite achieve workability: so I put them away. Hence the title for this final working, for at that time, early in my composer's journey, I was still in the process of escaping from the styles and musical habits of the past in order to find my own authentic voice.

In 2011 serendipity turned up the sketches: I immediately perceived the string quartet form as ideal, and worked the ideas into fruition. It is somewhat traditional in form, cast in 4 movements. As I redrafted and completed it I was aware of the references to the past (not totally in my awareness in the 1980s), so we could say it's a Post-modernist work, critiquing itself! I believe it will be enjoyable nonetheless! *[premiered October 2012, Jaqueline du Pré Music Building, Oxford.]*

      **i. Larghetto, Moderato, Poco allegro - 4.56'**

      **ii. Scherzo - 2.31'**

      **iii. Lento, non troppo - 3.26'**

      **iv. Allegro giocoso, Misterioso movimento, Cantabile, Allegro**
                                        **- 8.14'**

THAT IS THEN FOLLOWED BY **String Quartet no.4**: *Touching the Deep.*

In July 2013 I dreamed some truly angelically beautiful music! On waking I said to myself "How am I going to manifest *that*!"—possibly I may have got close here and there . . .

It picks up its ethos from the early 17thC attitude indicated by the word 'melancholia', not to be interpreted in the modern sense of pathological sadness, an unwanted state of being requiring therapy: Historically it means rather a deep feeling state that engaged with the world as found. John Dowland's music, perhaps, is the epitome of those times.

Earlier Albrect Dürer depicted the state in the engraving *Melencolia* 1 as an awaiting of inspiration. Later, the German *Sturm und Drang* movement took up the attitude, typified by Goethe's *The Sorrows of Young Werther.* And naturally the outlook was integral to the *Romantic Movement,* with such exemplars as Keat's *Ode to Melancholy.* Part of the human condition, this psycho-cultural attitude appeared also elsewhere, and elsewhen. *[This performance was its first.]*

> i. Wistfulness - teneramente, affetuoso - 5.03'
>
> ii. Dancing Life's Tears - sonoro movimento - 4.15'
>
> iii. Melancholia - soave, dolente - 4.03'
>
> iv. Finale: Praeludium - semplice - 1.49'
>
> v. Caritas ad infinitum - deciso - 5.02'

THEN ON THE WEB PAGE: clementjewitt.co.uk/recordings-2/

Firstly three songs, again with the Astaria String Quartet and Wendy Nieper. They are excerpted from *The Night Sea: aspects of an ordinary life'*, a 50' song cycle which was written for Wendy, with a male voice choir and chamber orchestra, which awaits a full performance. These three songs were lightly scored in the original, so lent themselves to string quartet arrangements. They are in the order of the full score. The Whitman and Eberhart settings are the first two, the latter reinforcing the former. *'The Coming of Light'* comes near the end of the cycle, after a plethora of life's experiences have been encountered, and is followed by the last setting, not performed as yet, e.e.cummings wonderful sonnet *'i thank You God for most this amazing day'*. So death, metaphoric if you will, precedes new life, growth of spirit or body or both occurring after meaningful life experiences.

### The Last Invocation (Walt Whitman)

At the last, tenderly,
From the walls of the powerful fortress'd house,
From the clasp of the knitted locks,
            from the keep of the well-closed doors,
Let me be wafted.

Let me glide noiselessly forth;
With the key of softness unlock the locks — with a whisper,
Set ope the doors O soul.

Tenderly — be not impatient,
(Strong is your hold O mortal flesh,
Strong is your hold O love).

*[Premièred May 2000, Magdalen College Recital Room, Oxford.]*

### Rumination (Richard Eberhart)

When I can hold a stone within my hand
And feel time make it sand and soil, and see
The roots of living things grow in this land,
Pushing between my fingers flower and tree,
Then I shall be as wise as death.
For death has done this, and he will
Do this to me, and blow his breath
To fire my clay, when I am still.

### The Coming of Light (Mark Strand)

Even this late it happens:
        the coming of love, the coming of light.
You wake and the candles are lit as if by themselves,

> stars gather, dreams pour into your pillows,
> sending up warm bouquets of air.
> Even this late the bones of the body shine
> And tomorrows dust flares into breath.

*[Both these were premiered April 2008, Holywell Music Room, Oxford.]*

FOLLOWING ALL THAT, SECONDLY, are a few songs, sung by various singers. These constituted a CD which I put together during 2021 as a 'thank you' to some of the singers, and a choir, who had agreed at various times to sing for me.

*NOTE: these were all recorded live during concerts, sometimes with somewhat inadequate recording equipment:  so the quality varies across the recordings, which please forgive.*

THE INDEFATIGABLE **Wendy Nieper** sings several, including three which she sang with the Astaria String Quartet (see above).  Here they are again, accompanied by pianist Kirsten Johnson, with additionally flutist Christopher Britton in *The Coming of Light.*

1st: *Rumination (Richard Eberhart)* - With Kirsten Johnston

The text here is above on the previous page.

2nd:  *Skins 20 (Charles Wright)* - with Kirsten Johnston

> You've talked to the sun and moon,
> Those idols of stitched skin, bunch grass, and twigs
> Stuck on their poles in the fall rain :
>
> You've prayed to Sweet Medicine;
> You've looked at the Hanging Road, its stars

The stepstones and river bed where you hope to cross;
You've followed the cricket's horn
To sidestep the Lake of Pain . . .

And what does it come to, Pilgrim,
This walking to and fro on the earth, knowing
That nothing changes, or everything:
And only, to tell it, these sad marks,
Phrases half-parsed, ellipses and scratches across the dirt

It comes to a point. It comes and it goes.

3rd: *The Coming of Light (Mark Strand)* - With Kirsten Johnson & Christopher Britton. This text is on the previous page.

4th: *Come With Me (Milton Godfrey)* - with Kirsten Johnson. This is Milton's nostalgic remembrances of his early life in Jamaica. I met him when we were both taking a music degree in Birmingham:

Come with me where
The blue sea lashes
The shore and palm trees
Bow to the sun;
Where children laugh
And play in warmth
And the sky masquerade
As if hurricanes were
Things of the past

Come with me where
Brightly coloured clothes
And smiling faces,
Butterflies, and things,
Are painted against
A skyline with rainbows
In the distance, costumed
For the occasion.
Come with me.

Come with me where
Fireflies glow at night,
Birds and insects send
Signals; where moonbeams
Add mystique to the night,
And sounds are suppressed
By occasional silence.

Come with me where
Distant clouds form
On a humid day, from
Countless waves breaking
The surface of the sea,
Churning, rippling, until
Disappearing on the
Shoreline.

Come with me where

The sun, so near,
It seems, can be touched.
And we are touched
By a fading moon that

Demands attention while
It waits for return of the Sun

**5th: *He Would Send Me Running (Marion Griffin)*,** the 2nd movement of String Quartet no.1, with its accompaniment reduced from string quartet to piano - Kirsten Johnson

He would send me
running
Up grassy banks
Ahead of him.
If I had taken a tumble
He would have been there
To break my fall
To kiss my grazes.

And so I ran
Made the top
Laughed and panted
While he
Took the last stride
To join me
And take my hand again.

And before we take leave of Wendy, there are two more songs:

**6th: *The Harvest Bride (Christina Edwards)*** - with Kirsten Johnson. Quite a long time ago, Christina gave me this poem written in red on a decorative slightly *art nouveau* style background, suggesting I might like to set it. A lovely gift. After writing the song, I asked her if she would write a programme note. She declined, staunchly, to de-mystify her poem, and instead gave me this precisely accurate sentence: *"Before the triumph of the Long Night comes the final ecstasy of flowering."*

Golden Moon of Plenty
Hark the Earth's lament
Weeping for the Harvest
Bride's
Ecstatic Sacrament

Burnished Moon of Blood
Hark the Hunter cries...
I come, my Lord, adorned
For bliss and Sacrifice.

Midwinter Moon of Ice,

| Beneath thy deathly shine | Dance I with my Lord of Night In union sublime. |

7th: *Three Hokku on Time (composers text)* - with Christopher Britton. Conceived originally for Wendy as a duet for voice and flute. The traditionally sparse texts (as in *haiku*) are surrounded by vocal and flutic modal elaborations, some partly improvised.

| Enfolded time is<br>At the moment of embrace:<br>So ageless both be.<br><br>Unending time is<br>At the facing of yourself: | So agéd all be.<br>Unheeded time is<br>At the last calm acceptance:<br>Enough just to be |

NOW WE HAVE **Sarah Verney**, pianist, singer, and at the time of these recordings, music therapist living in Birmingham, England. The reader may recall seeing her referred to in earlier chapters.

*The Last Invocation (Walt Whitman)* - with the Antara String Quartet, comprised of Birmingham Conservatoire students, led by Kelly McCusker, who later played 2nd fiddle with the Astaria quartet (see above).

| At the last, tenderly,<br>From the walls of the powerful<br>    fortress'd house,<br>From the clasp of the knitted<br>    locks, from the keep of the<br>    well-closed doors,<br>Let me be wafted.<br><br>Let me glide noiselessly forth; | With the key of softness unlock<br>    the locks—with a whisper,<br>Set ope the doors O soul.<br><br>Tenderly—be not impatient,<br>(Strong is your hold O mortal<br>    flesh,<br>Strong is your hold O love). |

*But a Part of It All (James Kavanaugh)* - With the string trio from the Antara Quartet, led by Kelly McCusker.

1. Sadness is but a part of it all
   Coming so relentlessly in the
           morning,
   The offscouring of dreams.
   Why do you run?
   The birch tree does not run
   Stripped of his leaves by the
   cold       winds.
   Waiting silently all winter,
   without complaint
   Standing knee deep in the snow,
           without motion.
   He knows the cold will go away
   That the sun will warm the
   grass    green
   And give back his leaves
   And lure back his birds.

   He knows that only fools are not
           sad.

2. Life has its beginnings, coming
           at intervals.
   Time to start anew.
   None is first or last, save birth
           and death.
   Nor can we decide
   Which is most significant,
   Transforming, or long enduring.
   It only matters that each
           beginning, like spring,
   Be given its due.
     To nourish the earth for
           flowers
     To respect sun and rain for
           fertility.

AND NOW **Marianne Lihannah,** a versatile Danish mezzo-soprano performing and recording in the UK as a solo singer. She is accomp-anied with piano (1st song) and clarinet (2nd) both by **Matthew Heyse-Moore.**

*Save Now We Pray (bell hooks).* From *A Woman's Mourning Song.*

During a train journey I was struck by this poem by 'bell hooks' (pen name of Gloria Jean Watkins), and drafted the entire setting before the train arrived! It became my '7 bar blues'!

i want to go down
once more to the river
hear them black angels
sing hosanna
see those bodies go down
hear them hallelujah cries
amen and thank you jesus
i want to go down

into the dark and muddy water
hear them voices
moaning low praying sounds
to suffer surrender be free
to suffer surrender be free
to suffer surrender be free
to suffer surrender be free
i want to go down


## If You Came (Ruth Pitter)

If you came to my secret glade
Weary with heat
I would set you down in the
shade
I would wash your feet.

If you came in the winter, sad,
Wanting for bread,
I would give you the last that I
had,
I would give you my bed.

But the place is hidden apart
Like a nest by a brook;
And I will not show you my
heart
By a word, by a look.

The place is hidden apart
Like the nest of a bird;
And I will not show you my
heart
By a look, by a word.


AND FINALLY, A CHORAL PIECE conducted by **Giles Turner,** with the East Midlands choir **Kingfisher Chorale,**.

### Invocations to Archangels (composer's text).

Uriel, Uriel, Uriel, Fire of God,
Aid us at our waking
And at our rising up:
Fill us with your fire
That we may face our day
And live our lives, Uriel.

Gabriel, O messenger, O man of
God,
Flow through us at the
noontide

That we may feel, and hope.
Ah, Gabriel,
As you protect all sleeping
babes
Nurture with your loving care
Our unawakened selves,
O Gabriel, Gabriel.

Angel of the spirit of Man,
Namèd 'God heals', (Raphael,
Raphael)

Mediate at our eventides
Resting from our journey.
Raphael, Help us as we strive
To weigh up day and night,
To balance all our lives.
O Raphael,
Breathe into us, O Raphael,
The healing breath of God.

Míchäel, Míchäel,
Leader of the Heavenly hosts,
Guardian of the faithful,
Be with us at our sleeping.
Míchäel, in this your era,

Grant us dreams that we may
wake
To use our thoughts
With wisdom and with care,
In harmony with all humanity.

Archangels, Archangels,
With all your angel hosts,
Your healing work through us
That we may dedicate our lives
In this sad world,
To healing hates and fears.
*Archangels, Archangels.*

# Bibliography

Baron-Cohen, Simon & John E. Harrison (eds) 1997. *Synaesthesia: Classic and contemporary readings.* Blackwell

Beament, James 2001. *How We Hear Music: The relationship between music and the hearing mechanism.* Boydell Press.

Bentov, Itzhak 1978. *Stalking the Wild Pendulum: On the mechanics of consciousness.* Wildwood Hse

Campbell, Don G. 1989. *The Roar of Silence: Healing powers of breath, tone and music.* Quest.

Campbell, Joseph 1976(1959). *The Masks of God: Creative mythology.* Rev. Viking Penguin

Chinmoy, Sri 1995. *The Source of Music: Self-expansion through spiritual music and mantras.* Blue Beyond Books

Clayton, Martin 2000. *Time in Indian Music: Rhythm, metre and form in North Indian rāg performance.* Oxford University Press.

Cousto, Hans 1988. *The Cosmic Octave: Origin of harmony.* Life Rhythm

Cytowic. Richard E. 1997 *Synaesthesia: Phenomenology and neuropsychology - a review of current knowledge* – IN Baron-Cohen & Harrison. *Synaesthesia*

D'Angelo, James 2005. *The Healing Power of the Human Voice.* Healing Arts Press.

Eliade, Mircea 1959. *The Sacred and the Profane: The nature of religion.* Harcourt Brace

Gardner, Kay 1990. *Sounding the Inner Landscape: Music as medicine.* Caduceus Publ.

Godwin, Joscelyn 1987. *Harmonies of Heaven and Earth: The spiritual dimension of music from antiquity to the avant-garde.* Thames & Hudson

Hansen, George P. 2001. *The Trickster and the Paranormal.* Xlibris

Harvey, Jonathan 1999. *In Quest of Spirit: Thoughts on music.* U. Cal Press, with CD

Hill, Gareth S. 1992. *Masculine and Feminine: The natural flow of opposites in the psyche*. Shambhala

Hindley, Geoffrey 1997. *Keyboards, Cranks and Communication: The musical mindset of Western technology*. in *ICON, Journal of the International Committee for the History of Technology*, Vol.3

Hodgkinson, Tim 1996. *Siberian Shamanism and Improvised Music*. Contemporary Music Review Vol.14, Parts 1-2 (59-66).

Hunt, Valerie V. 1996. *Infinite Mind: Science of the human vibrations of consciousness*. 2nd ed. Malibu Publ

Jung, Carl Gustav. CW 9ii. (Collected Works vol.9 part 2) *Aion*.

Kenny, Carolyn Bereznak (ed.) 1995. *Listening, Playing, Creating: Essays on the power of sound*. State University of New York Press.

Knox, Sarah S. 2023. *Bringing the Biomedical Paradigm into Consonance with Quantum Reality*. Paradigm Explorer No.140, pp3-8

Leeds, Joshua 2001. *The Power of Sound: How to manage your personal soundscape for a vital, productive and healthy life*. Healing Arts Press.

Lerdahl, Fred 1988. *Cognitive Constraints on Compositional Systems*. IN Sloboda, John A. 1988

Luria, Alexander R. *Synaesthesia* (reprinted from *The Mind of a Mnemonist*) IN Baron-Cohen & Harrison. *Synaesthesia*

McClellan, Randall 1991. *The Healing Forces of Music: History, theory and practice*. Harper Collins

McGilchrist, Iain 2009. *The Master and his Emissary: The divided brain and the making of the Western world*. Yale.

Neher, Andrew 1962. *A Physiological Explanation of Unusual Behaviour in Ceremonies Involving Drums*. Human Biology Vol.34 No.2 (151-160)

Oliveros, Pauline 1990. *Introduction* to Gardner, Kay. *Sounding the Inner Landscape: Music as medicine*. Caduceus Publications.

Paton, Rod 2001. *Structures of Trust: Improvisation and communication with music*. Music & Psyche Journal Issue 1 (8-18)

Petsche, Helmuth *et.al.* 1993. *EEG Coherence and Musical Thinking*. Music Perception Vol. 11, No.2 (117-151)

Rauscher, Frances et.al. 1993. *Music and Spatial Task Performance*. Nature Vol. 365, 14th October

Rawson, Philip 1996. *Laya in Indian Music: Monody and the shapes of time*. Contemporary Music Review Vo.14, Parts 3-4 (35-46)

Reichel-Dolmatoff, Gerado 1997. *Rainforest shamans: Essays on the Tukano Indians of the Northwest Amazon*. Themis

Rodwell, Mary 2017. *The new human: Awakening to our cosmic heritage*. New Mind Publ.

Roney-Dougal, Serena, n.d. *Walking between the worlds* (Lecture series). Tape

Rowell, Lewis 1992. *Music and Musical Thought in Early India*. University of Chicago Press.

Ruud, Even 1995. *Improvisation as a Liminal Experience: Jazz and music therapy as modern "rites de passage"*. IN Kenny 1995.

Scheiby, Benedikte 1995. *Death and Rebirth Experiences in Music and Music Therapy*. IN Kenny 1995.

Scott Peck, M. 1993. *Stages of Community Building*. IN Whitmyer, Claude (ed.). *In the Company of Others: making community in the modern world*. Putnam/Perigee Books.

Shlain, Leonard 1998. *The alphabet versus the Goddess: male words and female images*. Viking

Sloboda, John A. (ed.) 1988. *Generative Processes in Music: The psychology of performance, improvisation and composition*. Clarendon Press.

Steiner, George 1989. *Real Presences*. U. of Chicago Press.

Steiner Followers 1951. *Music*. Anthroposophical Publishing House

Taylor, Steve 2021. *Extraordinary Awakenings: When trauma leads to transformation*. New World Library

Tilly, Margaret 1977, "The Therapy of Music," *Jung Speaking*, eds. William McGuire & R.F.C. Hull. Princeton: Princeton University Press.

Tippett, *Sir* Michael 1974. *Moving into Aquarius*. Paladin Books

Watson, Lyall 1976. *Gifts of Unknown Things*.  Hodder & Stoughton

Whitmont, Edward C. 1993  *The Alchemy of Healing: Psyche and soma*.
    North Atlantic Books

Whitmyer, Claude (ed.) 1993.  *In the Company of Others: making
    community in the modern world*.  Putnam / Perigee Books

Zuckerkandl, Victor 1973.  *Man the Musician*. (Sound & symbol, Vol 2).
    Princeton UP

# Index of names

pages

*17th Century*, England     14

Abram, David, phenomenalist     68

Ancient Greek Architecture     50

*Antara Quartet*     193/4

*Aquarian age*     33, 120

*Astaria String Quartet*     143ff, 184/5, 188

*Australia*     72

*Authors  see  Writers - Poets*

Bach, J.S.     15/6, 26, 44, 52/3, 63, 70, 117

Bags, Sydney, writer     161

*Banisteriopsis, psychotropic vine*     130

Bardsley, Mike, harpsichordist/pianist     5, 22, 145

Bartok, Bela, composer     32, 44, 53, 54, 50

*Bavarian bierkellers*     70

BBC Light Orchestra     36

Beethoven, Ludwig van     15, 25, 39, 53/4, 117

Bentov, Itzhak, inventor     123/4

Bergson, Henri, philosopher     45, 53

Biberian, Gilbert, composer & guitarist     145

*Birmingham Conservatoire*     5, 7, 22, 140

Bonacci, Leonardo, mathematician     49

Boulez, Pierre, composer     28, 44, 63 ff

Bristol University     22

Britton, Christopher     144, 190/1, 193

Brookman, Bill, multi-instrumentalist     145

*Buddhism, Mahayana*     83

Burke, John, composer     150 ff

Burniston, Andrew (Fred), Jung scholar     30

Burrell, Diana, composer and teacher     161/2

Burton, Deirdre, wisewoman                                    165
Byrd, William                                                  30
Campbell, Joseph, mythologist                              115 ff
*Canada House, London*                                         34
Casals, Pablo                                               6, 46
*Chipping Norton, Oxfordshire*                            14, 129
Chopin, Frédéric                                          49, 54
Clayton, Martin, writer on music                               45
*Common Ground Report*                                      87 ff
*Composers merely named*: Bartok, Berio, Birtwistle, Britten, Debussy,
    Holst, Ligeti, Mahler, Messiaen, Schönberg, Shostakovich,
    Stockhausen, Stravinsky, Takemitsu, Webern              26/7
    Carter, Boulez, Murail                                   42
    Berlioz, Stravinsky                                     121
    Boulez                                                   44
    Dunstable                                                48
    Liszt, Rimsky-Korsakov, Scriabin, Messiaen              128
    Mendelssohn                                              20
    Messiaen                                                 69
    Powers                                                   28
    Tippett                                                  25
Cone, Edward, writer on music                                  81
Conway, Clive, flutist                                        129
Cummings, E.E., poet                                          189
Cytowic, Richard, neurologist                               130/1
*Dartington college*                                           30
Davies, Maxwell, composer                                      72
Daw, Stephen, reporter                                        164
Dawes, Joycelin, Spiritual Inquiry initiator                87 ff
Debussy, Claude                                                70
Descartes, René                                               113
Dunstable, John                                                72

| | |
|---|---|
| Dürer, Albrect | 188 |
| Eliade, Mircea, historian of religion | 90, 112 |
| *Elizabethans on sonority* | 72 |
| Elson, Shulamit, writer | 162 |
| *Ernst Bloch Lectures* | 82 |
| *Franco-Germanic rivalry* | 70 |
| *Gaunt's House* | 2 |
| Garcia Conway Duo | 129 |
| *German Jews in New York* | 21 |
| Gilde, Sean, cellist | 144 |
| Goethe, Johann Wolfgang von | 188 |
| Handel, George Frideric | 117 |
| Hansen, George, sociological writer | 33 |
| Harvey, Jonathan, composer | 31, 77 ff |
| Haydn, Joseph | 9 |
| Head, Raymond, all-round musician | 143, 163/4 |
| Heidegger, Martin | 84 |
| Heyse-Moore, Matthew, pianist & clarinetist | 141 |
| Hillman, James, psychologist | 112 |
| Hodgkinson, Tim, improviser | 93 |
| Howard, Katherine, painter | 163 |
| Hunt, Valerie, researcher of consciousness | 126 |
| Husserl, Edmund, phenomenalist | 68 |
| Hyder, Ken, improviser | 93 |
| *Jaqueline Du Pre Music Room* | 143 ff |
| Johnston, Kirsten, pianist | 190/2 |
| Jung, C.G. | 6, 32, 120 |
| Keats, John | 188 |
| *Kingfisher Chorale* | 195/6 |
| Kivy, Peter, writer on music | 81 |
| Lang, Corinne, singer | 165 |
| *Leicester Mercury, newspaper* | 30 |

Lendvai, Ernö                                              54
Léonin, 12thC composer                                  49, 57
Lerdahl, Fred, writer on music                             43
*Les Six (French Modernists)*                              70
Lihannah, Marianne, singer                          141, 194/5
Lloyd-Gonzalez, Steven, conductor                          34
*London Conservatoires*                                    22
*London Jung Club*                                         30
London, North, in WW2                                      17
*London Sinfonietta*                                       31
McCusker, Kelly, violinist                              193/4
MacDonald, Calum, *Tempo* editor                        140/1
Mahler, Gustav, *9th Symphony*                             79
Maslow, Abraham, psychologist                              80
Mendelssohn, Felix                                         35
Merleau-Ponty, Maurice                                     68
Mitchell, Madeleine, violinist                            141
Morley, Christopher, reporter                             165
*Moulin Rouge*                                             70
Mozart, Wolfgang Amadeus                                  117
*Music & Psyche*, group improvisors                7, 83ff, 140
*Musicians see Composers*
Nabokov, Vladimir, novelist                               128
Nares, Susan, musician & therapist                         87
Nieper, Wendy, singer          34, 143/4, 183/5, 188/93
Nordoff-Robbins School                                     76
Oliveros, Pauline, musician                                92
*Orkney, UK*                                               72
*Orlando Quartet*                                          29
*Painters merely named*:  Kandinsky, Hockney              128
*Participative Spiritual Inquiry*                        73/89
Paton, Rod, musician & teacher         87, 94, 99, 100, 161

*Pavlova Wind Quintet*                                       143
Pérotin, fl c.1200, composer                              49, 57
Petsche, Hellmuth                                            66
*Phenomenalists*: Husserl, Merleau-Ponty, Abram             68
*Poets merely named*: Basho, Rimbaud, Baudelaire           128
Potter, Mitch, reporter                                    164
Poole, Geoffrey, pianist & composer                     54, 141
Powers, Anthony, composer                                  30/1
*Quartetto Italiano*                                          7
Rawson, Philip, writer                                      46
*Renaissance*                                               113
Robinson, Oliver, psychologist                             101
*Roman Catholicism*                                    57, 72, 83
Rowell, Lewis, writer on music                             45/6
*Royal Festival Hall, London*                                 5
Scarlatti, Domenico                                         63
Schönberg, Arnold, composer                                 32
Scott Peck, M., psychiatrist                                96
*Severnside Composers Alliance*                            141
Shankhar, Ravi, sitarist                                   5, 8/9
Shlain, Leonard, writer on cultures                        118
*Shoreham, Kent*                                             14
*Society for the Promotion of New Music (SPNM)*         29, 31
*Spanish Guitar Centre, London*                             14
Steer, Maxwell, composer                               87, 150 ff
Steiner, George, literary critic                           105
Steiner, Rudolf                                        64, 74, 117
Strachan, Gordon, writer & teacher                          37
Stravinsky, Igor, composer                                  43
*Sturm und Drang*                                          188
Szigeti, Joseph, violinist                                 6, 46
Takács-Nagy, Gábor, chamber musician                       184

| | |
|---|---:|
| Takemitsu, Toru, composer | 129 |
| Taylor, Steve, psychologist | 20 |
| Thoma, Sue, acquaintance | 163 |
| Tilly, Margaret, pianist & music therapist | 6 |
| Tippett, Michael, composer | 32 |
| Turner, Giles, conductor | 195 |
| Verney, Sarah, singer & therapist | 34, 64, 87, 193/4 |
| *Visnudharamorttara Purānā* | 41 |
| Wagner, Richard | 60 |
| Watson, Lyall, explorer & writer | 126/7, 131 |
| Wilkinson, Delyth, singer & psychotherapist | 34 |
| Williamson, Malcolm, composer | 72 |
| *World Music* | 71 |
| *World War II (WW2)* | 17/18 |
| *Writers merely named*: William Golding, James Joyce, Thomas Mann, Robert Pirsig, Shakespeare | 121 |
| Basho, Rimbaud, Baudelaire, Nabokov | 128 |
| Zuckerkandl, Victor, writer on music | 81 |

Printed in Great Britain
by Amazon